Table of Contents

Introduction 2

The Golden Fish (A Russian Folktale) 4
recall details; draw conclusions; use inference; word meanings; sequence events; long/short i; antonyms; adjectives

The Goose That Laid Golden Eggs (An Aesop Fable) 11
recall details; draw conclusions; word meanings; adjectives; sequence events; th; plural forms; personal narrative

A Bell for the Cat (An Aesop Fable) 17
recall details; draw conclusions; word meanings; long e; suffixes er/est; nouns; follow directions; use creative thinking

The Tortoise and the Eagle (An African Fable) 23
recall details; draw conclusions; word meanings; sequence events; long vowel sounds; articles a/an; true or false

The Pancake (A Scandinavian Folktale) 30
recall details; draw conclusions; real and make-believe; word meanings; pronouns; sequence events; short vowel sounds; compound words

The Grasshopper and the Ants (An Aesop Fable) 37
recall details; draw conclusions; make a prediction; word meanings; antonyms; gr/dr; word family ack; add suffixes ed/ing; syllables

The Frog Prince (A Folktale from Germany) 44
recall details; draw conclusions; word meanings; adjectives; silent letters; ô; sequence events; cause & effect

The Monkey and the Crocodile (A Folktale from India) 51
recall details; draw conclusions; word meanings; multiple meanings; sequence events; final y; homophones; true or false

The Crow and the Pitcher (An Aesop Fable) 58
recall details; draw conclusions; personal narrative; word meanings; multiple meanings; long o; ough; past tense; base words; problems & solutions; critical thinking

Momotaro, the Peach Boy (A Folktale from Japan) 64
recall details; draw conclusions; make a prediction; word meanings; sequence events; ed/d/t; word families (each, own); present tense; adding es

The Boy Who Went to the North Wind (A Scandinavian Folktale) 71
recall details; draw conclusions; word meanings; ow (ou, long o); compound words; homophones; verbs; sequence events; personal narrative

The Fox and the Stork (An Aesop Fable) 78
recall details; draw conclusions; use inference; word meanings; oo; prefix un; classify

The Four Musicians (A German Folktale) 83
recall details; draw conclusions; word meanings; oo; contractions; synonyms; analogies

The Shoemaker and the Elves (A German Folktale) 89
recall details; draw conclusions; personal narrative; word meanings; multiple meanings; long a; suffixes less/ful/ly; figures of speech; write an interview

The Rabbit That Ran Away (A Fable from India) 96
recall details; draw conclusions; make a prediction; personal narrative; word meanings; er; syllables; cause & effect

The Little People (A Native American Fable) 102
recall details; draw conclusions; personal narrative; word meanings; synonyms; long vowel sounds; homographs; rhyming words; suffixes er/est

The Crow and the Peacock (A Folktale from China) 108
recall details; draw conclusions; personal narrative; word meanings; silent letters; soft/hard g; suffixes less/ful; similes; syllables

The Boy Who Cried Wolf (An Aesop Fable) 114
recall details; draw conclusions; word meanings; prefixes un/pre/under; categorization; synonyms/antonyms; homophones

The Sun and the Wind (An Aesop Fable) 119
recall details; draw conclusions; creative thinking; word meanings; synonyms; ou; articles a/an; cause & effect; personal narrative

How the Princess Learned to Laugh (A Folktale from Poland) 124
recall details; draw conclusions; personal narrative; word meanings; gh; soft/hard c; past/present tense; write a letter

The Tiger and the Big Wind (A Folktale from Africa) 131
recall details; draw conclusions; personification; word meanings; word family eat; contractions

Answer Key 137

Introduction

Types of Stories

- folktales
- fables

Ways to Use the Stories

1. Directed lessons
   - with small groups of students who are reading at the same level
   - with an individual student

2. Partner reading

3. With cooperative learning groups

4. Independent practice
   - at school
   - at home

Things to Consider

1. Determine your purpose for selecting a story—instructional device, partner reading, group work, or independent reading. Each purpose calls for a different degree of story difficulty and support.

2. A single story may be used for more than one purpose. You might first use the story as an instructional tool, have partners read the story a second time for greater fluency, and then use the story at a later time for independent reading.

3. When presenting a story to a group or an individual for the first time, review any vocabulary that will be difficult to decode or understand. Many students will benefit from a review of the vocabulary page and the questions before they read the story.

Types of Skill Pages

Four or five pages of activities covering a variety of reading skills follow each story:

- comprehension
- vocabulary
- phonics
- structural analysis
- parts of speech
- record information

Ways to Use Skill Pages

1. Individualize skill practice for each student with tasks that are appropriate for his or her needs.

2. As directed minilessons, the skill pages may be used in several ways:

   - Make a transparency for students to follow as you work through the lesson.

   - Write the activity on the board and call on students to fill in the answers.

   - Reproduce the page for everyone to use as you direct the lesson.

3. When using the skill pages for independent practice, make sure that the skills have been introduced to the reader. Review the directions and check for understanding. Review the completed lesson with the students to determine if further practice is needed.

The Golden Fish

A Russian Folktale

In a land far away lived a poor old man and his wife. They lived in an old shack with a crooked roof. The old shack was on a small hill near the sea. Their only food was the fish that the old man caught.

Each morning the old man took his fishing net down to the sea. He would throw the net into the cool, blue water. Then he would pull it back in filled with fish. One day, when he pulled the net back in, he saw something shiny. It was a golden fish. The golden fish began to speak. It begged the old man to throw it back into the water. "If you let me live, I will grant you a wish."

The kind old man didn't ask for anything. He just put the golden fish back into the water. When he got home, the old man told his wife what had happened. She was very angry. "Go back and ask the fish for a loaf of bread for us to eat!" she shouted.

The old man did as his wife asked. He caught the golden fish again. "Please may I have a loaf of bread," he asked the fish. When he got home, a loaf of bread was on the table.

Folktales & Fables • EMC 757

The old man's wife said, "The fish gave us one wish. Maybe he will give us more." The next day, she told her husband to ask the fish for a new washtub. He did as his wife asked. When he got home, there was a new washtub in the front yard. But his wife was not happy.

Each day she wanted more. She wanted a new house. She wanted to be rich. She wanted to be queen. Each time the golden fish granted her wish.

But even being queen did not make the old woman happy. She sent her husband to the golden fish one last time. She wanted to rule the land and sea and everything that lived there. The old man caught the golden fish and made the wish.

"Go home," said the golden fish. "Your wife will get what she should have."

When the old man got home, he saw his wife dressed in rags. She was standing inside the old shack. And there was not even a loaf of bread left to eat.

Name _____

Questions about
The Golden Fish

1. Where did the old man and his wife live?

_____

2. How did the old man catch fish?

_____

3. Tell two ways the golden fish was different from other fish.

   a. _____

   b. _____

4. What was the wife's first wish?

_____

5. What was the wife's last wish?

_____

6. Why did the golden fish take everything away from the old man and his wife?

_____

●●● Think About It ●●●

Write three things you learned about the old man from this story.

1. _____

2. _____

3. _____

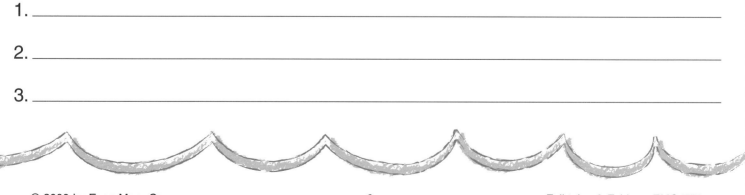

Name _____

What Does It Mean?

Write each word by its meaning.

begged	loaf	sea	shiny
grant	poor	shack	washtub

1. an old broken-down house _____

2. the ocean _____

3. bright _____

4. asked for something _____

5. to give what is asked for _____

6. bread baked in one large piece _____

7. a place to wash clothes _____

8. not having much money or many things _____

• • • Where Was It? • • •

Match:

1. loaf of bread   in the fishing net

2. shiny, golden fish   inside the old shack

3. wife dressed in rags   on a small hill near the sea

4. old shack   on the table

Name _____

The Old Man's Wife

The fish granted the old man's wife many wishes. List in order the things she wanted.

1. _____

2. _____

3. _____

4. _____

5. _____

6. _____

Draw:

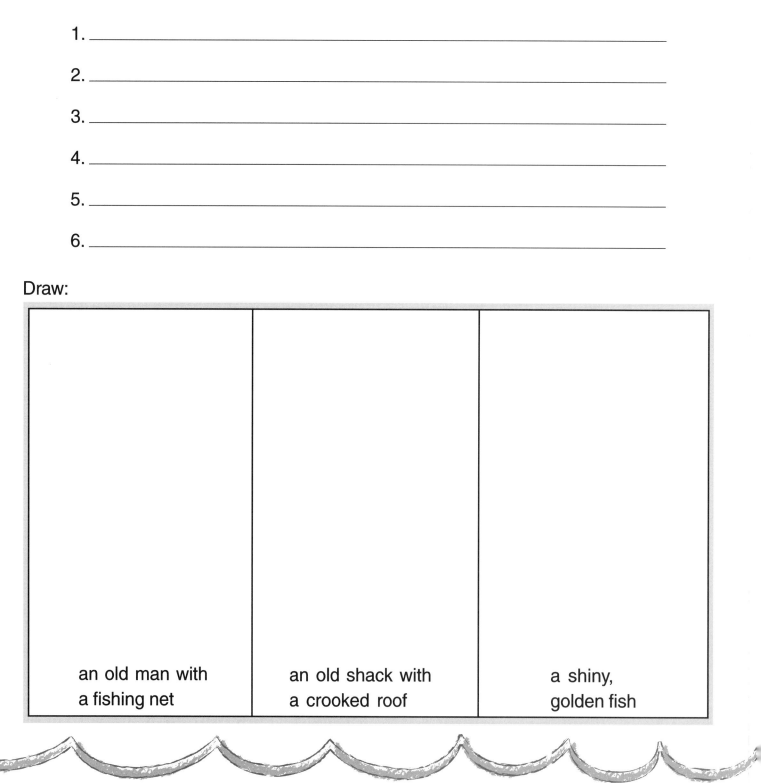

| an old man with a fishing net | an old shack with a crooked roof | a shiny, golden fish |

Folktales & Fables • EMC 757

Name _____

Long *i* and Short *i*

Read the words. Write each word in the correct box.

| lived | find | will | wife | shiny | give | rich | why |
| kind | wish | fish | his | my | tiny | into | time |

Long **i** Words	Short **i** Words
_____ _____	_____ _____
_____ _____	_____ _____
_____ _____	_____ _____
_____ _____	_____ _____

● ● ● Make New Words ● ● ●

You can change the first letter of many words to make new words.
Change these words. Then read the new words to someone.

kind ___f___ind   **c**atch ___m___atch

1. wish _____ish

2. will _____ill

3. land _____and

4. man _____an

5. net _____et

6. cool _____ool

7. fold _____old

8. may _____ay

9. but _____ut

   Folktales & Fables • EMC 757

Name _____

Adjectives

An **adjective** is a word that describes someone or something.
Circle the adjectives in this list.

shiny	shack	golden	talking
bread	poor	table	catch
old	greedy	angry	kind

Use the circled words to describe the following:

1. _____, _____ man

2. _____, _____ fish

Write a sentence that describes you.

_____

_____

● ● ● Opposites ● ● ●

Match the words that are opposites.

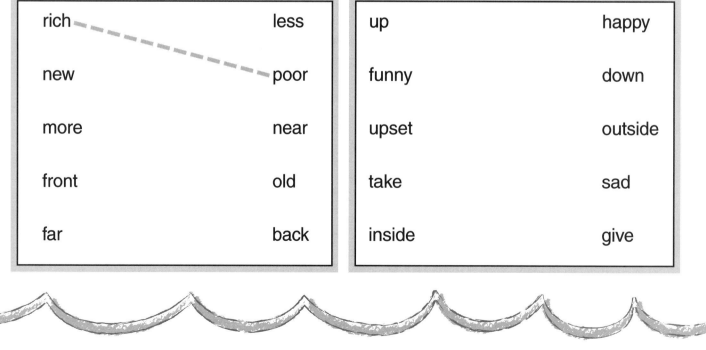

rich	less
new	poor
more	near
front	old
far	back

up	happy
funny	down
upset	outside
take	sad
inside	give

The Goose That Laid Golden Eggs

An Aesop Fable

A farmer and his wife went to a fair in the next town. They wanted to buy a new goose to eat the weeds in their garden. They found a large, plump goose and took her home. They didn't know that this was their lucky day.

The next morning, the farmer's wife went to collect eggs. She found a big yellow egg in the goose's nest. She picked up the strange egg and took it to her husband. "Look at this egg the goose laid," she said. "It is very heavy and very yellow."

The farmer took the egg. His mouth fell open. "This egg is made of gold," he said.

The goose laid a golden egg every day. The farmer and his wife grew very rich from selling the eggs. And they grew very, very greedy.

"Let's cut open the goose. Then we can get all of the golden eggs at one time," said the farmer. But when they cut the goose open, there was no gold. The goose was just like all geese inside. Now the greedy farmer and his wife had no more golden eggs. And they didn't have a goose to eat the weeds in the garden.

The farmer and his wife kept buying geese. They wanted to find a new goose that laid golden eggs. But they were out of luck.

Name _____

1. Why did the farmer and his wife buy a goose?

_____

2. How did the farmer and his wife become rich?

_____

3. Why did the farmer cut open the goose that laid golden eggs?

_____

4. What did the farmer find when he cut open the goose?

_____

5. What lesson did the farmer and his wife learn?

_____

• • • How Did They Feel? • • •

Color the face to show how the farmer and his wife felt.

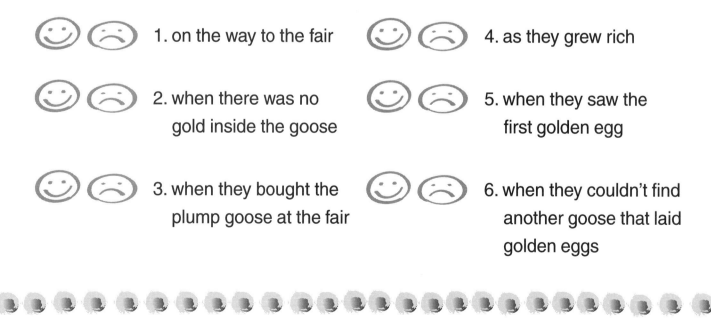

1. on the way to the fair

2. when there was no gold inside the goose

3. when they bought the plump goose at the fair

4. as they grew rich

5. when they saw the first golden egg

6. when they couldn't find another goose that laid golden eggs

12 Folktales & Fables • EMC 757

Name _____

What Does It Mean?

Match each word to its meaning.

1. wife   a place to buy and sell farm products and animals

2. fair   round and full; a little bit fat

3. weeds   a married woman

4. plump   wanting more than your share

5. strange   wild plants growing where they are not wanted

6. greedy   unusual; not seen before

● ● ● Words That Describe ● ● ●

Write the words that describe each person or thing in the correct box.

lucky	plump	yellow	large	rich
magical	heavy	greedy	golden	

_____	_____	_____
_____	_____	_____
_____	_____	_____

Name _____

What Happened Next?

Cut out the sentences.
Paste them in order.

1. [ ]

2. [ ]

3. [ ]

4. [ ]

5. [ ]

6. [ ]

✂ -

They grew rich selling the golden eggs.

The goose was just like all the geese inside.

The farmer's wife found an egg made of gold in the goose's nest.

The greedy farmer cut open the goose to get all of the gold at one time.

A farmer and his wife went to the fair. They bought a goose to eat weeds in their garden.

Now the greedy farmer and his wife had no more golden eggs.

 Folktales & Fables • EMC 757

Name _____

The Sounds of *th*

Circle the words that have the **th** sound you hear in **the**.

Make an **X** on the words that have the **th** sound you hear in **thing**.

they	mouth	that	think	their
thin	this	with	another	

Use the words above to complete these sentences.

1. The farmer went _____ his wife to the fair.

2. _____ went to the fair to buy a goose.

3. The farmer's _____ fell open when he saw the golden egg.

4. Why did he _____ gold was inside the goose?

5. The farmer and his wife wanted to buy _____ goose.

● ● ● More Than One ● ● ●

one    **more than one**

Add **s** to make more than one.	Add **es** to make more than one.	Write the special word for more than one.
1. egg _____	1. dish _____	1. goose _____
2. nest _____	2. box _____	2. tooth _____
3. dog _____	3. wish _____	3. man _____
4. hat _____	4. brush _____	4. mouse _____

Name _____

Read and Draw

Draw a large golden egg in the nest.

Draw a plump goose sitting on the egg in the nest.

Draw yourself finding the golden egg.

● ● ● A Golden Egg ● ● ●

Write about what you would do if you found a golden egg.

I would _____

_____

_____

_____

A Bell for the Cat

An Aesop Fable

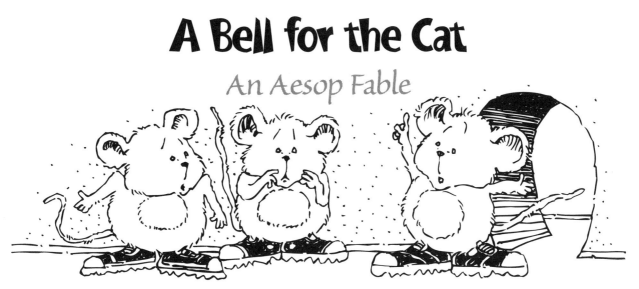

The cat was causing a terrible problem. It was catching and eating all of the mice! "What can we do? What can we do?" cried the mice.

One of the older mice called a meeting. "We need to find a way to solve this problem," said the mouse. "How can we keep that hungry cat from catching any more of us?"

The mice talked and talked and talked. No one could think of a good way to solve the problem. At last, a little mouse stood up. He said, "I know what to do. The cat can sneak up on us because it is so quiet. We should put a bell around the cat's neck. Then we could hear when it is coming and run for cover."

"Hoorah!" shouted the other mice. "We're saved! We're saved! We'll put a bell on the cat!"

As the mice shouted with joy, a quiet old mouse stood up. The old mouse said, "I think a bell on the cat is a good plan. It would give us a chance to escape that hungry cat. But, tell me, just who will put it there?"

The room became very quiet. Slowly each mouse left the room. No one wanted to bell the cat.

Folktales & Fables • EMC 757

Name _____

Questions about
A Bell for the Cat

1. What was the mice's problem?

_____

2. Why did the mice have a meeting?

_____

3. What was the little mouse's plan?

_____

4. How would putting a bell on the cat help the mice?

_____

5. What happened when the old mouse asked who would put the bell on the cat?

_____

6. What lesson did the mice learn?
   a. A plan isn't any good if it can't work.
   b. It is good to have a plan.

● ● ● Think About It ● ● ●

Imagine you are one of the mice in the story. Think of a plan to save the mice.

_____

_____

_____

_____

Name _____

What Does It Mean?

Use these words in place of the underlined words.

terrible	bell the cat	sneak
escape	run for cover	meeting

1. The mice <u>got together to talk</u>.

   The mice had a _____.

2. The mice wanted to <u>get away</u> from the cat.

   The mice wanted to _____ from the cat.

3. The mice had to <u>find a place to hide</u>.

   The mice had to _____.

4. The mice planned to <u>put a bell around the cat's neck</u>.

   The mice planned to _____.

5. It was an <u>awful</u> problem.

   It was a _____ problem.

6. The cat would <u>creep</u> up on the mice.

   The cat would _____ up on the mice.

Name _____

The Sounds of Long e

Read the long **e** words.

ea	ee	e
eating	meeting	she
sneak	need	he
peach	keep	we

Circle the missing word.

1. The cat was _____ mice.   eeting   eating

2. The mice had a _____.   meating   meeting

3. Is _____ your sister?   she   shee

4. Bob tried to _____ a cookie.   sneak   sneek

● ● ● Adding Endings ● ● ●

	Add **er**.	Add **est**.
tall	tall_____	tall_____
old	old_____	old_____
young	young_____	young_____

Write the missing ending.

1. The old_____ mouse called a meeting.

2. How much old_____ are you than your sister?

3. The young_____ mouse had a plan.

4. That baby is young_____ than I am.

5. The giant was much tall_____ than Jack.

Name _____

Nouns Can Name Things

Circle the nouns.

mouse	room	hungry	quiet
shout	bell	neck	cookie
hooray	old	cat	escape
mice	book	little	hole

Use the circled words above to complete these sentences.

1. A hungry _____ chased a little gray _____.

2. The students hurried to their class_____ when the

   _____ rang.

3. What kind of _____ do you like for dessert?

● ● ● ● ● ● ● ● ● ● ● ● ● ● ● ● ● ● ● ●

Look around the classroom.
List 10 nouns naming things you see.

1. _____   6. _____

2. _____   7. _____

3. _____   8. _____

4. _____   9. _____

5. _____   10. _____

   Folktales & Fables • EMC 757

Name _____

Belling the Cat

Follow these directions:

1. Color the mice brown.

2. Draw a bell hanging around the cat's neck.

3. Color the cat yellow with orange stripes.

4. Circle the mice peeking out of the hole.

5. Count the mice you see in the picture.
   (Be careful! Some are hiding.)

I counted _____ mice.

                   Folktales & Fables • EMC 757

The Tortoise and the Eagle

An African Fable

Eagle spent his time in the clouds. Tortoise spent his time on the ground. So the two didn't meet often.

One day Eagle went to visit Tortoise. Frog had told him that Tortoise was kind to his guests. Eagle wanted to see if this was true. It was! Tortoise asked Eagle to come in and fed him a tasty meal.

The food was so good that Eagle came back again and again. Every visit he ate all of Tortoise's food. But Eagle never invited Tortoise to his home.

One day Frog heard Eagle talking to himself. Eagle said, "Ha! I've eaten Tortoise's food many times. But he can't reach my home to eat mine."

Frog thought, "Tortoise is my friend. I will go tell him what Eagle is doing."

So Frog went to Tortoise's house. He said, "Eagle is laughing about never having to feed you. He knows you can't reach his home in the treetop. But I have a plan. Here's what you can do." And he told Tortoise the plan.

The next day Eagle came again. Tortoise said, "Please let me give you a gourd full of food. It is a gift for your wife."

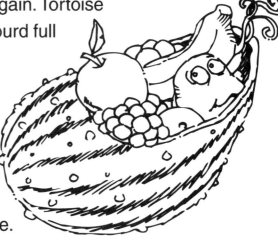

While Eagle ate his meal, Tortoise went into the kitchen. He climbed into a large gourd and his wife piled food on top of him so he couldn't be seen. She gave the gourd to Eagle.

When Eagle reached home, he put the gourd on the floor. He was surprised to see Tortoise roll out of it. "I have come to visit you," said Tortoise. "When do we eat?"

The selfish Eagle became angry. He said, "You'll be the only meal here!" He tried to peck Tortoise's hard shell. He didn't hurt Tortoise. He just hurt his own beak.

"I can see you are not my friend after all," said Tortoise. "Take me home." And he grabbed Eagle's leg.

Eagle flew up into the sky and tried to shake Tortoise off. "I'll throw you to the ground. You'll smash into little bits!" he cried.

But brave Tortoise kept his hold on Eagle's leg. At last Eagle gave up. Eagle took Tortoise home and let him go.

As Tortoise walked into his house he looked back at Eagle. He said, "Friends share with each other. You have been selfish and unkind. Don't come back again."

Name _____

Questions about
The Tortoise and the Eagle

1. Why did Eagle go to visit Tortoise?

_____

2. How could you tell that Tortoise was kind to his guest?

_____

3. How could you tell that Eagle was selfish?

_____

4. What was Frog's plan to trick Eagle?

_____

_____

5. Tell two ways Eagle tried to hurt Tortoise.

_____

_____

6. How did Tortoise manage to get back home?

_____

_____

● ● ● **Think About It** ● ● ●

What did Tortoise learn about Eagle?

_____

What did Eagle learn about Tortoise?

_____

Name _____

What Does It Mean?

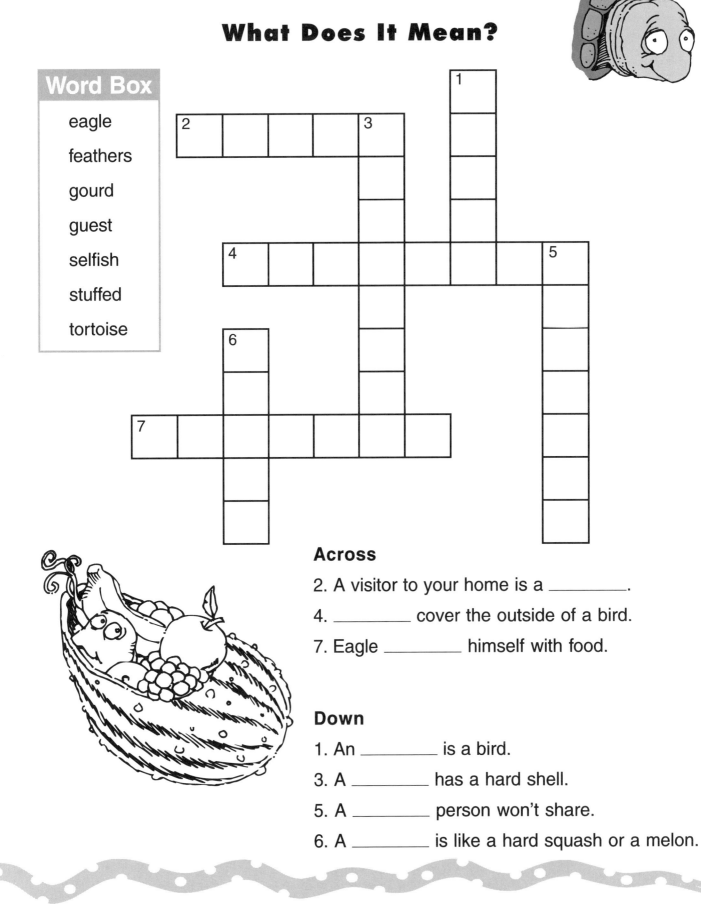

Word Box

- eagle
- feathers
- gourd
- guest
- selfish
- stuffed
- tortoise

Across

2. A visitor to your home is a _____.

4. _____ cover the outside of a bird.

7. Eagle _____ himself with food.

Down

1. An _____ is a bird.

3. A _____ has a hard shell.

5. A _____ person won't share.

6. A _____ is like a hard squash or a melon.

Name _____

What Happened Next?

Number the pictures in the order in which they happened.

27   Folktales & Fables • EMC 757

Name _____

Long Vowel Sounds

Read each word. Write the long vowel sound you hear.

1. eagle _e_

2. home _____

3. time _____

4. tree _____

5. day _____

6. use _____

7. kind _____

8. meal _____

9. my _____

10. go _____

11. cute _____

12. came _____

13. ate _____

14. wife _____

15. beak _____

16. throw _____

17. gave _____

18. sky _____

• • • Using *a* and *an* • • •

We use **a** and **an** before a noun.

An is used before words starting with a vowel sound.

A is used before words starting with a consonant sound.

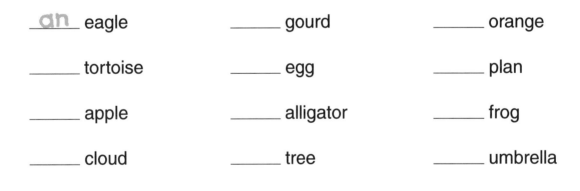

_an_ eagle

_____ tortoise

_____ apple

_____ cloud

_____ gourd

_____ egg

_____ alligator

_____ tree

_____ orange

_____ plan

_____ frog

_____ umbrella

Name _____

Who Said It?

Write the correct name on each line.

Eagle   Frog   Tortoise

1. "Eagle is laughing at you," said _____.

2. "Ha! I've eaten Tortoise's food, but he can't eat mine," said _____.

3. "You have been selfish and unkind," said _____.

4. "Here's what you can do," said _____.

5. "I'll throw you to the ground," said _____.

6. "When do we eat?" said _____.

● ● ● **Is It True?** ● ● ●

Check the facts that are true about a tortoise and an eagle.

	Tortoise	**Eagle**
1. It has feathers.		
2. It is alive.		
3. It has a hard shell.		
4. It can fly.		
5. It walks on four legs.		
6. It lives on land.		
7. It must eat to stay alive.		
8. It has a strong beak and sharp claws.		

The Pancake

A Scandinavian Folktale

Long ago and far away there was a farm wife. She had seven hungry children. One morning she said, "I think I'll cook a large, tasty pancake for breakfast." Her children smelled the pancake cooking and came to beg for a bite.

"Give me a bite of pancake, Mother. I am so hungry," said her first child.

"Dear Mother," said the second.

"Dear, sweet Mother," said the third.

"Dear, sweet, nice Mother," said the fourth.

"Dear, sweet, nice, pretty Mother," said the fifth.

"Dear, sweet, nice, pretty, good Mother," said the sixth.

"Dear, sweet, nice, pretty, good, kind Mother," said the seventh.

"I will give you a bite when the pancake is done," said their mother.

All at once, the pancake jumped off the griddle. It rolled through the door and down the hill.

"Stop, pancake!" shouted the farm wife. She ran after the pancake with the griddle still in her hand. Her seven hungry children followed as fast as they could go.

"Stop, pancake!" they all screamed. But the pancake rolled on and on until they couldn't see it.

The pancake rolled on until it met a hen. "Good day, Pancake," said the hen. "Don't roll so fast. Rest awhile and let me eat you."

Folktales & Fables • EMC 757

"I ran away from the farm wife and her seven hungry children," said the pancake. "I will run away from you, too, Henny Penny." And the pancake rolled on. Soon it met a duck.

"Good day, Pancake," said the duck. "Don't roll so fast. Stop a little and let me eat you."

"I ran away from the farm wife and her seven hungry children and from Henny Penny," said the pancake. "I will run away from you, too, Ducky Lucky." And the pancake rolled on. Soon it met a pig.

"Good day, Pancake," said the pig.

"The same to you, Piggy Wiggy," said the pancake.

"Don't be in such a hurry," said the pig. "Let's travel together to the other side of the forest. It's not safe in there."

So they went along together. Soon they came to a brook. Piggy Wiggy swam across the brook. But the poor pancake couldn't get over. "Sit on my snout and I'll carry you over," said the pig.

The pancake did not stop to think. It just hopped up onto Piggy Wiggy's snout. As quick as a wink the clever pig swallowed the pancake. That is the end of the pancake. And that is the end of our story.

Folktales & Fables • EMC 757

Name _____

Questions about
The Pancake

1. Why did the farm wife have to make such a large pancake?

   _____

2. List the six words the children called their mother when they were begging for food.

   _____   _____   _____

   _____   _____   _____

3. How did the pancake move from place to place?

   _____

4. What animals did the pancake meet?

   _____   _____   _____

5. Why did the pancake run away from everyone?

   _____

6. How did Piggy Wiggy trick the pancake?

   _____

   _____

● ● ● Real and Make-Believe ● ● ●

Circle the things that are real.

Make an **X** on the things that are make-believe.

A mother can cook a pancake.   A pig can eat a pancake.

Children do beg for a bite to eat.   A pancake can roll down the road.

A pancake can jump off a griddle.   Children can run after their mother.

A hen can talk like a person.   A pancake can jump onto the snout of a pig.

 Folktales & Fables • EMC 757

Name _____

What Does It Mean?

Match:

griddle — to ask for something

beg — smart or skillful

hungry — a flat pan used for cooking

snout — needing food

clever — in a big hurry

brook — front part of a pig's head

quick as a wink — a little stream of water

● ● ● Pronouns ● ● ●

Write a pronoun for each underlined noun.

it	he	she	they
me	we	her	them

1. <u>Mother</u> cooked a tasty pancake. _____

2. The children followed their <u>mother</u>. _____

3. <u>The pancake</u> rolled on and on. _____

4. <u>The children</u> begged for a bite of pancake. _____

5. The pancake ran away from <u>a mother and her children</u>. _____

6. "Let <u>duck</u> eat you," said Ducky Lucky. _____

What Happened Next?

Draw what happened next.

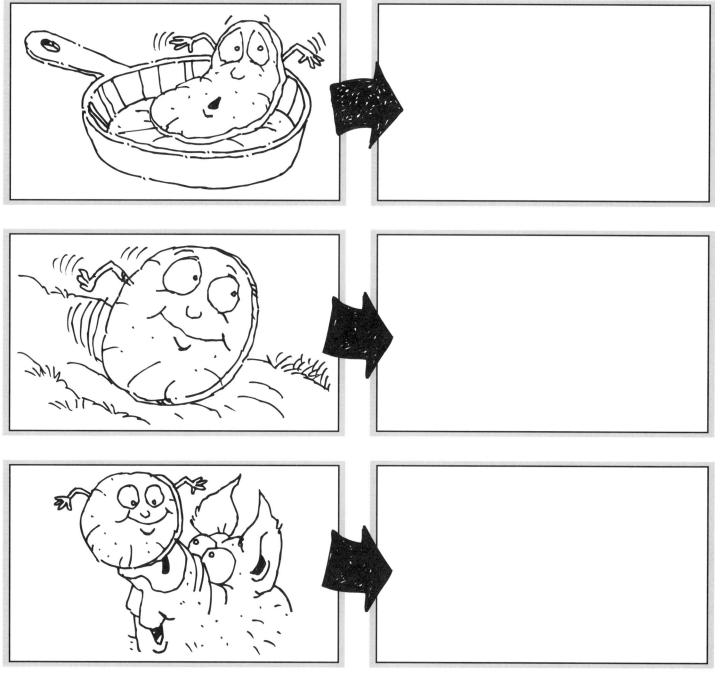

Name _____

Sounds of Short Vowels

Write each word in the correct box with its short vowel sound.

smell	had	stop	but	give
fast	will	beg	on	duck
hen	run	ran	quick	not
griddle	hopped	stamp	that	rest
stuck	end	wink	block	such

a	e	i	o	u

••• Compound Words •••

A **compound word** is made of two smaller words.

pan + cake = **pancake**

Match a word in each column to make compound words. Write the new words on the lines.

rain	boy	_____
butter	bow	_____
pea	nut	_____
cow	fly	_____

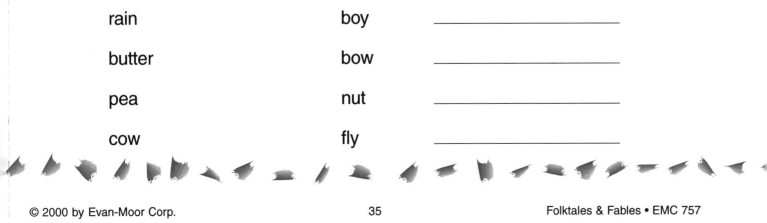

The Farm Wife's Children

Cut out the seven children. Paste them in the correct order.

The third child is the tallest.

The fifth child is holding a cat.

The first child has on glasses.

The seventh child is the shortest.

The fourth child has on a funny hat.

The second child is wearing boots.

The sixth child has black hair.

The Grasshopper and the Ants
An Aesop Fable

It was summertime and the days were warm and bright.
The field was filled with insects. Bees and butterflies were flitting
from flower to flower. Dragonflies were flying by. A grasshopper was
hopping about the field. He saw a line of ants passing by. The
ants were carrying seeds. The grasshopper said,

"Come play with me,
let's have some fun."

But the busy ants kept moving as they called to him,

"We can't stop now,
work must be done."

The grasshopper spent his days hopping along and singing.
Every day he saw ants carrying seeds
to the nest. And every day he said,

"Come play with me,
let's have some fun."

And every day the ants called to him,

"We can't stop now,
work must be done."

Folktales & Fables • EMC 757

One day the grasshopper asked an ant, "Why are you working so hard? You could be playing in the warm summer sun."

"I am helping to store food for the winter," said the ant. "I think you should do the same."

"Why bother about winter now?" asked the grasshopper. "There is plenty of food to eat." The grasshopper hopped away to play. The ant went back to its work.

When winter came, the ants were never hungry. They ate the food they had stored during the summer. But the poor grasshopper could find nothing to eat. "Now I see why the ants worked so hard," cried the grasshopper. "When you have a lot, you should save some for later."

Name _____

Questions about
The Grasshopper and the Ants

1. What were the days like in the summertime?

_____

2. What did grasshopper do all day?

_____

3. What did the ants do all day?

_____

4. Why were the ants working so hard?

_____

5. What happened to the grasshopper when winter came?

_____

6. What lesson did the grasshopper learn?

_____

7. What do you think the grasshopper will do next summer?

_____

_____

● ● ● Think About It ● ● ●

Do you think the ants should have shared their food with the grasshopper?
Why or why not?

_____

_____

_____

Name _____

What Does It Mean?

Write each word by its meaning.

| bright | save | store | summer | busy |
| plenty | warm | field | insects | winter |

1. seasons of the year _____ _____

2. all you need of something _____

3. small six-legged animals _____

4. shiny _____

5. to keep some for later _____ _____

6. a place with wild grasses and few trees _____

7. having a lot to do _____

8. having a little bit of heat _____

• • • Opposites • • •

Match the words that are opposites.

summer	day
work	short
ask	play
stay	winter
night	go
tall	answer

sad	over
awake	small
under	early
late	happy
now	asleep
large	then

 Folktales & Fables • EMC 757

Name _____

The Sounds of *gr* and *dr*

Add **gr** to these words. Read the words to a friend.	Add **dr** to these words. Read the words to a friend.
_____in	_____ain
_____ain	_____ive
_____ay	_____op
_____ound	_____ummer
_____avy	_____eam

● ● ● A Word Family—*ack* ● ● ●

Add **ack** to make new words. Then use the words to complete the sentences.

b_____   bl_____

s_____   sh_____

t_____   st_____

cr_____   att_____

1. The old man and his wife lived in a _____.

2. I used a _____ to pin the paper to the wall.

3. The plate had a large _____ in it.

4. My dog is _____ with white spots.

5. Mom packed my lunch in a brown _____.

6. Put those books _____ on the shelf.

 Folktales & Fables • EMC 757

Name _____

Add Endings—*ed, ing*

Add endings to the words.

look	look**ed**	look**ing**

1. work   _____   _____

2. play   _____   _____

Add a letter and an ending.

beg	beg**ged**	beg**ging**

1. drum   _____   _____

2. stop   _____   _____

Change **y** to **i** and add **ed**.

try	tr**ied**

1. carry   _____

2. cry   _____

• • • How Many Syllables? • • •

Write the number of syllables after each word.

done _1_   **under** _2_   **dragonfly** _3_

grasshopper _____   hopped _____   carrying _____

line _____   butterfly _____   cried _____

beetle _____   should _____   answered _____

summer _____   busy _____   field _____

Name _____

Compare an Ant
and a Grasshopper

Same _____

_____

Different _____

_____

●●● Insects ●●●

Ants and grasshoppers are both insects.

Find them and the other insects in the word search.

grasshopper   honeybee

beetle   ladybug

butterfly   moth

ant   dragonfly

cricket

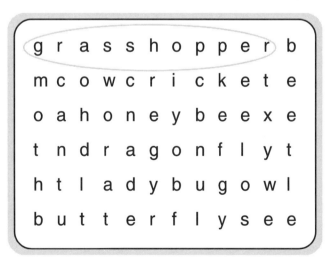

The Frog Prince

A Folktale from Germany

The king gave his youngest daughter a golden ball. It was her favorite toy. One day, as she was playing, the golden ball fell into a deep well. The princess sat by the well weeping. She heard someone say, "What is the matter, little one?" She looked up and saw a large, ugly frog.

"My golden ball has fallen down the well. I can't reach it," sobbed the princess.

"If you take me home and let me be your best friend, I will get the ball," said the frog.

"Oh, yes!" promised the princess. But as soon as the frog handed her the golden ball, she ran back to the castle.

"Wait for me!" shouted the frog as he hopped after her.

The princess ran into the castle and shut the door. She wanted to forget her promise to the frog.

That night at dinner, there was a knock at the door. It was the frog. The king asked the frog, "Why have you come to the castle?"

The frog told the king what the princess had promised him in return for his help. "Well," said the king, "she must do as she promised."

The frog hopped up next to the princess. He began to eat off her plate. When the princess started to complain, her father frowned and told her to be quiet.

After dinner the king told his daughter to take the frog to bed with her. She knew she had to obey her father. She did what he said, but she was not happy about it. The frog fell asleep on a pillow next to the princess.

When she woke up the next day, the first thing the princess saw was the frog. She cried out, "You slimy thing. Get off my bed!" and threw the frog against the wall.

Right before her eyes, the frog changed into a young prince. "Thank you for saving me," he said. "I was under a spell. I had to remain a frog until a princess kept her promise to me."

The king was happy that his daughter had learned to keep her promises. The prince was happy that he wasn't a frog. And the princess was happy that she no longer had to eat and sleep with a frog.

Name _____

Questions about
The Frog Prince

1. Describe the princess's favorite toy.

_____

2. Why did the princess need help from the frog?

_____

3. What did the frog want in return for helping the princess?

_____

4. How did the king help the frog get what it had been promised?

_____

5. What happened when the princess threw the frog against the wall?

_____

6. How did the princess help break the spell the prince was under?

_____

7. What do you think the princess will do the next time she makes a promise? Why?

_____

_____

••• Think About It •••

What made each character in the story happy?

1. King _____

2. Princess _____

3. Prince _____

Name _____

What Does It Mean?

Match each word to its meaning.

1. daughter   liked the most

2. favorite   to say that something is wrong; to find fault

3. weeping   to do as you are told

4. well   a girl child in a family

5. promise   crying

6. complain   to stay where you are

7. obey   a deep hole in the ground containing water

8. frown   to give your word; agree to do something

9. remain   an unhappy or angry look

● ● ● Adjectives ● ● ●

Match the adjectives to what they describe.

youngest

slimy

favorite

unkind

large

golden

Name _____

Silent Letters

The letter **k** is silent in words beginning with **kn**. Add **kn** to complete these words. Then draw a picture to illustrate each word.

_____ee	_____ight	_____ife

Read these words. Cross out the letters that do not make a sound.

1. knock	4. sigh	7. talk
2. comb	5. listen	8. wrote
3. knew	6. wring	9. kneel

● ● ● Spell ô ● ● ●

al–tall   **o**–got   **ol**–hollow   **aw**–crawl   **augh**–taught

Fill in the missing letters.

1. The princess s_____ an ugly fr_____g by the well.

2. The king gave a golden b_____l to his d_____ter.

3. The princess didn't keep her pr_____mise.

4. The fr_____g began to c_____l, "Stop! Stop!" as the princess ran away.

Name _____

What Happened Next?

Number the sentences in order.

_____ The frog slept on the princess's pillow.

_____ The frog went to the castle.

_____ The frog got the golden ball for the princess.

_____ The frog turned back into a prince.

_____ The frog ate from the princess's plate.

• • • Read and Draw • • •

the golden ball down the well	the frog knocking at the castle door
the frog eating off the princess's plate	the frog on the princess's pillow

Name _____

Cause and Effect

A **cause** is an event that makes something else happen.

The thing that happens is the **effect**.

Fill in the missing cause and effect below.

Cause	Effect
_____ _____ _____	The princess sat by the well weeping.
Cause	**Effect**
The princess promised to be the frog's best friend if he helped her.	_____ _____ _____
Cause	**Effect**
_____ _____ _____	The frog changed into a prince.

The Monkey and the Crocodile

A Folktale from India

A family of monkeys lived in a tree by a riverbank. A family of crocodiles lived in the river. The mother crocodile watched the monkeys for a long time. One day she said to her son, "My son, catch one of those monkeys for me. I want to eat its heart."

"How can I catch a monkey?" asked her son. "They are up in a tree and I am down in the water."

"You're a smart crocodile. I'm sure you can think of a plan," answered his mother.

The crocodile thought and thought. At last he had a plan. In the center of the river was an island. On the island were trees filled with ripe fruit. He would trick a monkey into coming down for some of the fruit.

"Little monkey," called the crocodile, "the fruit on the island trees is ripe now. Would you like some to eat?"

The monkey liked ripe fruit, but he couldn't swim. "How can I get across to the fruit?" asked the monkey.

"Hop on my back and I'll carry you across," said the crocodile.

The monkey was hungry, and wanted some of the fruit, so he jumped onto the crocodile's back.

Folktales & Fables • EMC 757

Halfway across the river, the crocodile dove under the water. When he came back to the surface, the monkey gasped for air. "Why did you take me under the water, crocodile?" he asked.

"My mother wants to eat a monkey heart," answered the crocodile. "I am going to drown you and take her your heart."

Thinking quickly the monkey said, "I wish you had told me you wanted my heart. I left it back home in my tree. If you want my heart, we must go back to get it."

"Very well," said the crocodile. "I'll take you back so you can get your heart and bring it to me. Then we'll go to the island."

Well, as soon as the crocodile came near land, the monkey jumped off his back. He climbed up into the high tree branches. "My heart is up here. If you want it, you will have to come up to get it," he called down to the crocodile.

The crocodile had to return home and tell his mother that he couldn't get a monkey heart. The monkey and his family soon moved to a new tree far away from the crocodiles.

Name _____

Questions about
The Monkey and the Crocodile

1. Where did they live?

   a. the crocodilefamily_____

   b. the monkey family _____

2. What did the crocodile mother want to eat?

   _____

3. How did the crocodile son plan to catch the monkey?

   _____

   _____

   _____

4. How did the monkey trick the crocodile?

   _____

   _____

   _____

5. What do you think happened when the crocodile son told his mother he couldn't get the monkey heart?

   _____

   _____

Name _____

What Does It Mean?

Write a word from the story after each meaning.

1. land surrounded by water
   _____

2. two words for the middle point
   _____

   _____

3. bananas, apples, and pears
   _____

4. the top of the water
   _____

5. to die under water because there
   is no air to breathe
   _____

● ● ● Words with More Than One Meaning ● ● ●

Fill in the correct circle.

1. In this story, **watch** means:

   ○ something used to tell time

   ○ to keep guard

   ○ to look at carefully

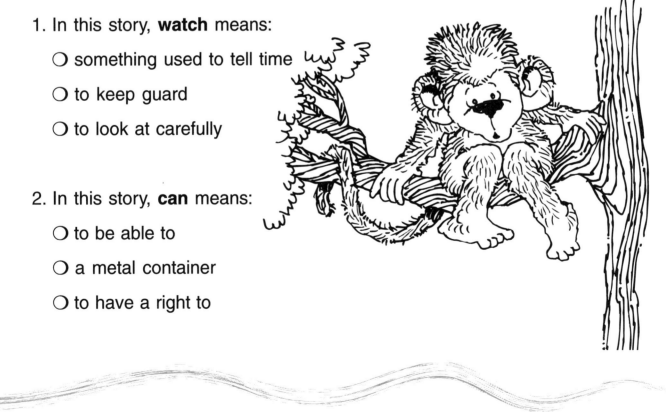

2. In this story, **can** means:

   ○ to be able to

   ○ a metal container

   ○ to have a right to

Name _____

What Happened Next?

Number the sentences in order.

_____ The crocodile son told a monkey about the ripe fruit in trees on the island in the river.

_____ The monkey found out the crocodile was after his heart. He said, "Too bad, I left my heart back in my tree."

_____ Mother crocodile wanted a monkey's heart to eat. She sent her son to get one.

_____ The crocodile son had to go home without a monkey heart for his mother.

_____ The crocodile took the monkey back to his tree to get his heart.

_____ The monkey hopped onto the crocodile's back to ride to the island.

_____ When they got near the tree, the monkey jumped off the crocodile's back. He climbed up the tree where he was safe.

Name _____

Y at the End

Read this list of words. Write the sound of the letter **y**.

1. quickly	_e_	5. monkey	_____
2. my	_____	6. why	_____
3. carry	_____	7. cry	_____
4. try	_____	8. greedy	_____

At the end of many one-syllable words, **y** says _____.

At the end of many two-syllable words, **y** says _____.

● ● ● Homophones ● ● ●

Homophones are words that sound alike but are spelled differently. They also have different meanings.

Circle the correct homophone to complete each sentence.

1. The _____ shone brightly in the sky.	son	sun
2. Ali _____ the answers to all the questions.	new	knew
3. Mark needs a lot of _____ to build a doghouse.	wood	would
4. Can I have _____ kinds of ice cream?	too	two
5. Would you like _____ of my popcorn?	some	sum
6. The lion hid in the tall grass waiting for its _____.	prey	pray
7. Kim found out that her dog had _____.	flees	fleas
8. In one _____ the train will leave the station.	our	hour

 Folktales & Fables • EMC 757

Name _____

Monkeys and Crocodiles

Make an **X** under the animal's picture if the fact is true.

1. It is an animal.	X	X
2. It is covered in fur.		
3. It has thick, scaly skin.		
4. It lives in trees.		
5. It spends most of the time in water.		
6. It uses sharp teeth and strong jaws to catch prey.		
7. It breathes air.		
8. It eats mostly plants.		
9. It uses its strong tail to help it swim.		
10. It lays eggs.		
11. Its babies are born alive.		
12. It has humanlike eyes and ears.		

The Crow and the Pitcher
An Aesop Fable

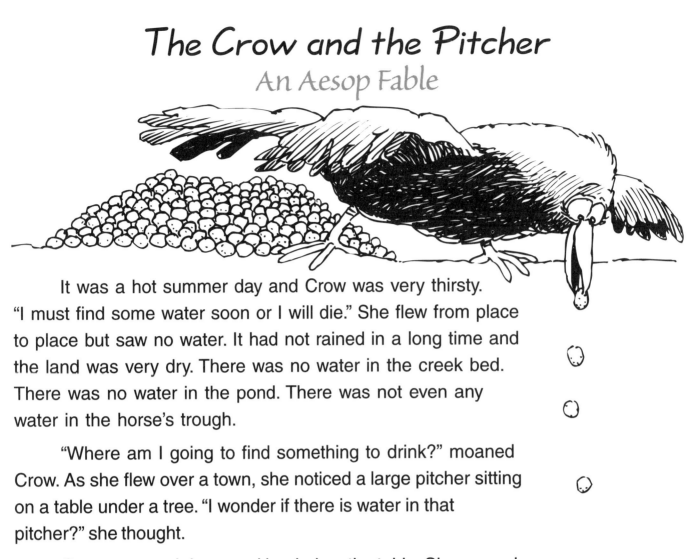

It was a hot summer day and Crow was very thirsty. "I must find some water soon or I will die." She flew from place to place but saw no water. It had not rained in a long time and the land was very dry. There was no water in the creek bed. There was no water in the pond. There was not even any water in the horse's trough.

"Where am I going to find something to drink?" moaned Crow. As she flew over a town, she noticed a large pitcher sitting on a table under a tree. "I wonder if there is water in that pitcher?" she thought.

Crow swooped down and landed on the table. She peered into the pitcher. Yes, there was water in it. "Oh, no!" she cawed. "There is only a little bit of water at the bottom!"

The thirsty bird tried to reach the water, but the neck of the pitcher was too small. She tried to tip the pitcher on its side so she could drink water as it spilled out. But it was too heavy. She was just wasting her time.

"I must think of a way to get to that water!" she cawed. Crow thought and thought. As she thought, she looked around. She noticed a pile of pebbles in the garden. This gave her an idea. One by one she picked up the pebbles and dropped them into the pitcher. Slowly the water rose to the pitcher's brim. Now Crow was able to drink until her thirst was gone.

Name _____

1. Crow was thirsty. What did she need to find?

_____

2. Write four places Crow looked for water.

_____   _____

_____   _____

3. Why couldn't Crow reach the water in the pitcher?

_____

4. Why couldn't she tip the pitcher over?

_____

5. What happened when she dropped pebbles into the pitcher?

_____

6. When did Crow get the idea to use the pebbles?

_____

_____

● ● ● Think About It ● ● ●

Write about a problem that you've had to solve.

My problem: _____

_____

How I solved it: _____

_____

Name _____

What Does It Mean?

Write each word next to its meaning. You will not use all of the words.

brim	wonder	peered
trough	swooped	moaned
pebbles	idea	creek

1. looked _____

2. flew down suddenly _____

3. the edge of a container _____

4. a plan _____

5. a small stream _____

6. small rocks _____

● ● ● Words with More Than One Meaning ● ● ●

Circle the correct meaning.

1. In this story, **bed** means:

   a. a piece of ground where plants are grown

   b. the ground under a body of water

   c. something to sleep on

2. In this story, **neck** means:

   a. the part of clothing that fits around your neck

   b. the part of the body between the head and shoulders

   c. the narrow part near the top of a pitcher or bottle

3. In this story, **pitcher** means:

   a. a container for holding and pouring liquids

   b. the baseball player who throws balls to the batter

Name _____

Long o

The long **o** sound is spelled in many ways.

o   **o—e**   **oa**   **ew**   **oe**   **ow**

Circle the words with the long **o** sound.

1. gone   stone
2. no   to
3. toast   tooth
4. out   oval

5. few   sew
6. crow   now
7. bomb   comb
8. globe   some

• • • One Sound of *ough* • • •

The letters **ough** are pronounced in many ways. In the following words, the letters make the sound of **ô** as in **thought**. Write **ough** on the lines.

f_____t   b_____t

s_____t   br_____t

Use the words you made above to complete these sentences.

1. Mr. Ramirez _____ hot dogs to the picnic.

2. When Cris fell and skinned her knee, she _____ back the tears.

3. The pirate _____ hidden treasure on the island.

4. The children _____ a special gift for their father's birthday.

Name _____

Past and Present

The **past tense** of an action word is used to tell that something already happened.

Yesterday I **played** in the park.

Write the past tense of these words.

drop   _____   think   _____

fly   _____   see   _____

begin   _____   give   _____

moan   _____   eat   _____

Use the words you made above to fill in the blanks.

1. The jet _____ over the tall mountain.

2. We _____ tuna sandwiches for lunch today.

3. I _____ the movie was too scary for my little brother to see.

4. A funny clown _____ balloons to the children at the circus.

• • • Base Words • • •

Write the base words on the lines. You may need to add or change a letter.

1. swooped   _____   6. slowly   _____

2. cried   _____   7. raised   _____

3. wasting   _____   8. dropped   _____

4. chases   _____   9. hopeless   _____

5. noticed   _____   10. hurried   _____

Name _____

Problems and Solutions

Fill in the boxes using information from the story.

Character _____

Problem _____

_____

_____

Solution _____

_____

_____

● ● ● Another Solution ● ● ●

The crow found one solution to the problem. Think up another way the crow might have reached the water in the pitcher. Write and illustrate your solution here.

_____

_____

_____

_____

_____

Momotaro, the Peach Boy

A Folktale from Japan

A kindly old man and his wife lived in a small house by a stream. Even though they were old, they still wished for a child.

One morning the old woman went to the stream to wash clothes. As she worked, she saw a large peach floating by. The old woman grabbed the peach and took it home for dinner.

When the old man began to cut the peach in half, he heard a loud "Pop!" The peach broke open and out jumped a plump, little boy. The old man and old woman were filled with happiness. "A boy of our very own!" said the old man. "Let's call him Momotaro, the Peach Boy."

Momotaro grew up to be brave and strong. Life was wonderful for the family until some terrible ogres moved onto a nearby island. The ogres came out at night to steal from the people in Momotaro's village.

One day Momotaro said to his parents, "I am going on a journey. I must stop the ogres." He packed a sword and some of his mother's wonderful dumplings.

The next morning, as his sad parents watched, Momotaro set off down the road. Soon he saw a dog resting by the side of the road. He gave the dog a dumpling and said, "Hello, dog. I need your help to fight the ogres. Will you come with me?" The dog followed Momotaro down the road.

As Momotaro and the dog passed by a grove of trees, they saw a monkey. Momotaro gave the monkey a dumpling. He said, "Hello, monkey. I need help from you to fight the ogres. Will you come with me?" The monkey leaped down from the tree and followed the dog and Momotaro.

As they crossed a river, the travelers heard a bird singing. Momotaro gave the bird a dumpling and said, "Hello, bird. I need help from you to fight the ogres. Will you come with me?" The bird joined the travelers on their journey.

After many days, the travelers reached the beach. They found a boat to take them to the island where the ogres lived. Momotaro said to the bird, "Fly ahead of us and tell the leader of the ogres that I have come."

The bird carried the message to the ogres' leader. Momotaro and the animals rushed in and began fighting the terrible ogres. The bird pecked their heads. The monkey jumped on their backs.

The dog bit their heels. Momotaro used his sword until he pinned the leader to the ground.

When the other ogres saw what had happened to their leader, they begged for mercy. They offered treasures to Momotaro if he would let them leave the country.

Soon Momotaro was on his way home with a cart filled with treasures and with the bird, dog, and monkey, too.

The old man and old woman wept with joy when they saw Momotaro returning.

Questions about
Momotaro, the Peach Boy

1. How did the old man and old woman get their son?

   _____

2. What happened when ogres moved onto a nearby island?

   _____

3. What two things did Momotaro take with him on his journey? How did he use them?

   _____

   _____

4. Name the three animals that went with Momotaro. How did each animal help fight the ogres?

   _____

   _____

   _____

5. How would you describe Momotaro?

   _____

● ● ● Think About It ● ● ●

Think of a good word to describe how the old couple felt:

1. when Momotaro set off to fight the ogres   _____

2. when Momotaro returned with the treasures   _____

Name _____

What Does It Mean?

Use these words to complete the following paragraphs.
You will use some words more than once.

| kindly | plump | traveled |
| ogre | journey | dumpling |

An ugly, old _____ complained, "I am so hungry I can hear my

stomach rumble. I would like a _____ like my mother used to make."

The _____ set off on a _____ to find someone to

make him a _____. He _____ many miles before coming

to a house. When he knocked, a _____ little lady opened the door and

smiled _____.

"I'm so hungry my stomach is rumbling. I need a _____,"

explained the _____. The little lady invited him in and began to cook.

She made a huge, tasty _____.

The _____ cleaned his plate and, with a big smile on his ugly

face, said, "Thanks, Mom!"

Name _____

What Happened Next?

Read each sentence. Write what happened next in the story.

1. The old man started to cut the peach in half.

_____

_____

2. Ogres moved onto an island near where Momotaro lived.

_____

_____

3. Momotaro saw a dog resting by the road.

_____

_____

4. Momotaro pinned the leader of the ogres to the ground.

_____

_____

5. Momotaro took the treasures and went home.

_____

_____

Name _____

The Sounds of *ed*

Write each word under the sound made by **ed**.

ed	d	t
_____	_____	_____
_____	_____	_____
_____	_____	_____
_____	_____	_____

followed	joined	leaped	waited
jumped	headed	shouted	begged
pecked	crossed	pinned	wanted

● ● ● Word Families ● ● ●

A word family is made up of words that are the same except for the beginning sounds. The words **night**, **sight**, and **fight** are in the same word family.

Use the clues to help you find members of the **each** word family.

1. a sandy place by the ocean _____each

2. to help someone learn _____each

3. to stretch your arm out for something _____each

4. a tasty fruit _____each

5. to give a sermon in church _____each

69   Folktales & Fables • EMC 757

Name _____

Present Tense Verbs

Add **s** or **es** to these verbs.

Then use them to complete the sentences below.

bite _____   take _____   watch _____

chase _____   push _____   wash _____

weep _____   break _____   wish _____

grow _____   steal _____   return _____

1. Marcos _____ home from school every day.

2. Karen's dog _____ the neighbor's cat.

3. It _____ a long time to learn how to be an astronaut.

4. Kai _____ his sled up the hill and rides it back down.

5. My brother _____ his cookies in half and then eats them.

6. Uncle Fred _____ football on television.

7. Kim's kitten _____ bigger every day.

8. Carl _____ his car every Saturday.

● ● ● Adding Endings ● ● ●

Change the **y** to **i** and add **es**.

1. worry _____   4. try _____

2. cry _____   5. hurry _____

3. carry _____   6. bury _____

70   Folktales & Fables • EMC 757

The Boy Who Went to the North Wind

A Scandinavian Folktale

A widow sent her son to the storehouse to fetch flour. As he came out of the storehouse, the North Wind blew the flour away.

The boy went back and got more flour. Again the North Wind blew it away. The boy got angry. He decided to go to the North Wind to get the flour back.

It was a long trip. At last the boy came to the North Wind's house. "Good day!" said the boy. He told the North Wind what had happened. "We don't have much to live on. If you blow away our flour, my mother and I will starve."

"I don't have your flour," said the North Wind. "But I'll give you a magic cloth. When you lay the cloth on a table and say the magic words, it will serve up good things to eat." And the North Wind told the boy the magic words.

The boy thanked the North Wind and started home. Along the way, he stopped at an inn for the night. When he was hungry, the boy laid the cloth on a table. He said, "Cloth, spread yourself." Soon the table was covered with good food.

While the boy was asleep, the landlord crept into his room. He took the magic cloth and left an ordinary one.

When the boy reached home, he went to show his mother what the North Wind had given them. But when he said the magic words, nothing happened. So he returned to the North Wind.

The boy said, "The cloth did not work. Give me back our flour."

"I don't have any flour to give you," said the North Wind. "You can take the fat ram in the field. If you say the magic words it will give you gold coins." And he told the boy the magic words.

The boy thanked the North Wind and started home. He stopped at the inn for the night. The boy paid for his room with gold coins that fell from the ram's mouth. While he slept, the landlord took the magic ram and left an ordinary one.

When the boy reached home the next day, he showed the ram to his mother. But when he said, "Ram, ram, make money," nothing happened.

Back he went to the North Wind. The North Wind said, "All I have left is this old stick. It can protect you." And the North Wind told the boy the magic words to use.

The boy stopped at the same inn. By now he knew what had happened to the cloth and the ram. Soon after supper, the boy lay down on his bed and pretended to be asleep.

The landlord waited for the boy to snore. Then he crept into the room and reached for the stick. The boy jumped up and called out, "Stick, stick, beat him!"

The stick began to beat the landlord. The landlord tried to run away, but the stick kept hitting him. "Please, stop it! I'll give back your cloth and ram!"

The boy said "Stick, stick, now stop!" Then he took the stick, the cloth, and the ram and went home.

The landlord had learned his lesson and was honest from that day on. And the widow and her son lived happily ever after.

 Folktales & Fables • EMC 757

Name _____

The Boy Who Went to the North Wind

1. Why did the boy go to the North Wind?

   _____

2. List the three things that the North Wind gave to the boy. Tell what kind of magic each one could do.

   _____

   _____

   _____

3. Why didn't the cloth and the ram work their magic when the boy got home?

   _____

4. How did the boy get the cloth and the ram back from the landlord?

   _____

   _____

5. What lesson did the landlord learn?

   _____

   _____

● ● ● Think About It ● ● ●

If you could choose only one thing from the story, would it be the magic cloth, the magic ram, or the magic stick? Think about it, and then explain on another sheet of paper why you chose that thing.

Name _____

What Does It Mean?—A Crossword Puzzle

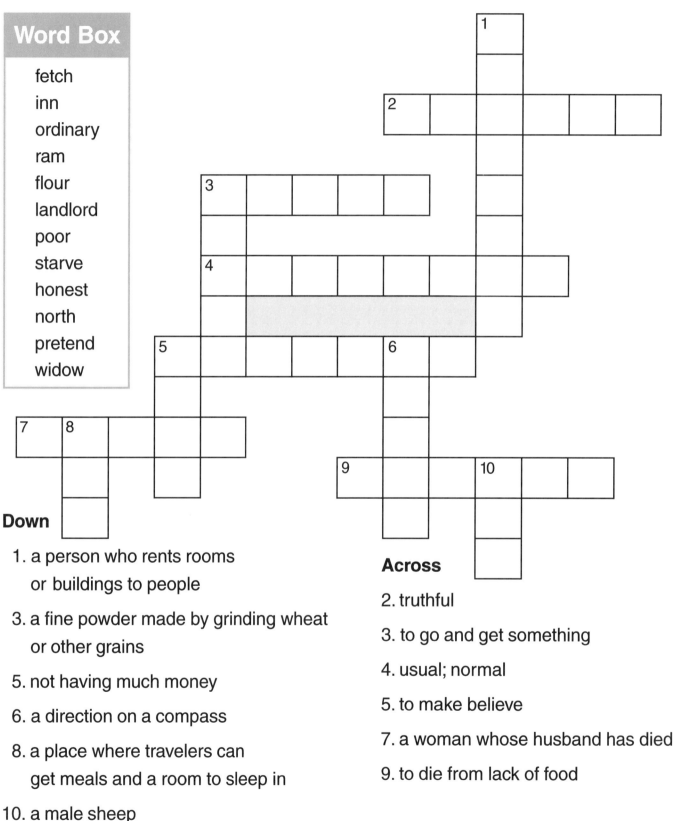

Word Box

fetch
inn
ordinary
ram
flour
landlord
poor
starve
honest
north
pretend
widow

Down

1. a person who rents rooms or buildings to people

3. a fine powder made by grinding wheat or other grains

5. not having much money

6. a direction on a compass

8. a place where travelers can get meals and a room to sleep in

10. a male sheep

Across

2. truthful

3. to go and get something

4. usual; normal

5. to make believe

7. a woman whose husband has died

9. to die from lack of food

Folktales & Fables • EMC 757

Name _____

The Sounds of *ow*

Read the words below. Then write them in the correct boxes.

ow	ō
_____ _____	_____ _____
_____ _____	_____ _____
_____ _____	_____ _____

flower	show	own	clown
widow	frown	tower	crowd
town	below	blow	row

● ● ● Compound Words ● ● ●

Use these words to make compound words.

store	land	table	night
cloth	mare	house	lord

1. _____   3. _____

2. _____   4. _____

Write one sentence using two of the words you made.

Circle the compound words.

_____

_____

Name _____

Homophones

Homophones are words that sound the same. They are not spelled the same, and they have different meanings.

Write the homophones for these words on the lines below.

flower	beet	in
burro	whole	peace
chews	dough	would

1. hole _____

2. piece _____

3. wood _____

4. flour _____

5. burrow _____

6. choose _____

7. inn _____

8. beat _____

9. doe _____

Correct the mistake in each sentence.

1. The gopher dug a whole in my garden. _____

2. Do you know how to make pizza doe? _____

3. The little burrow brayed, "Hee, haw!" _____

● ● ● Verbs ● ● ●

Verbs are action words. Circle the verbs in these sentences.

1. As the boy came out of the storehouse, the North Wind blew the flour away.

2. As the boy slept, the landlord crept into his room.

3. When the boy reached home, he showed the ram to his mother.

4. The boy lay down on the bed and pretended to be asleep.

What Happened Next?

Draw pictures to show what happened when the boy spoke the magic words.

The Fox and the Stork

An Aesop Fable

Long ago Fox and Stork were friends. One evening Fox invited Stork over for dinner. As a joke, he served only a shallow dish of thin soup. Fox lapped up the soup, but Stork could get only a few drops with her long, narrow bill.

"I am sorry that you do not like the soup," said Fox as he laughed behind Stork's back.

Stork did not complain or say that Fox was unfair. She just said, "Will you come to my house for dinner soon?" Fox quickly agreed to dine with Stork the following evening.

When Fox arrived at Stork's house, he smelled a delicious aroma. "I wonder what tasty meal Stork has cooked?"

Fox hurried to the table. Stork had made a stew filled with tiny bits of meat and vegetables. Stork brought the stew to the table in a tall jar with a narrow mouth. Now it was Stork's turn to laugh. She reached into the jar with her long, narrow bill and ate the delicious stew. Poor Fox sat by and watched. He could not get his snout far enough into the jar to reach the stew. He could only lick off the bits left on the mouth of the jar.

After dinner the hungry fox headed home. He knew that he could not blame Stork. He had been unkind to her. Fox had learned that you should treat others the way you want to be treated.

 Folktales & Fables • EMC 757

Name _____

Questions about
The Fox and the Stork

1. What joke did Fox play on Stork?

_____

2. How do you think Stork felt when she couldn't eat any soup?

_____

3. Why did Stork ask Fox to dinner after what he did to her?

_____

4. When Fox came to Stork's house for dinner, why couldn't he eat any of the stew she had made?

_____

5. What lesson do you think Stork was trying to teach Fox?

_____

_____

● ● ● Think About It ● ● ●

Can Fox and Stork still be friends after what happened in the story? Explain your answer.

_____

_____

_____

_____

What Does It Mean?—A Crossword Puzzle

Across

2. unjust; not fair

5. not deep

9. to be curious about

10. a flat dish

Down

1. not fat

3. not many

4. not wide

5. a bird with a long bill

6. to eat a meal

7. a smell; odor

8. a meal

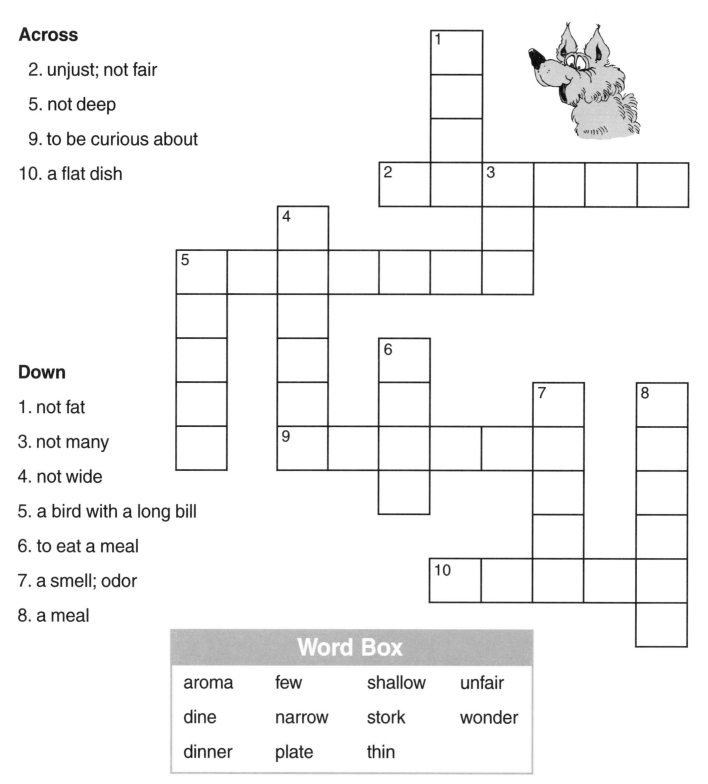

Word Box

aroma	few	shallow	unfair
dine	narrow	stork	wonder
dinner	plate	thin	

Folktales & Fables • EMC 757

Name _____

Spelling *oo*

Circle the letter or letters that say **oo** in these words.

soup	who	blue	few
stew	fruit	you	clue
soon	knew	two	suit

Fill in the missing letters to name the pictures.

s_____p   fr_____t   t_____

● ● ● The Prefix *un* ● ● ●

The prefix **un** means **not**. Add **un** to these words. Then use each new word in a sentence.

_____fair   _____kind   _____comfortable

1. _____

2. _____

3. _____

Name _____

Mammals and Birds

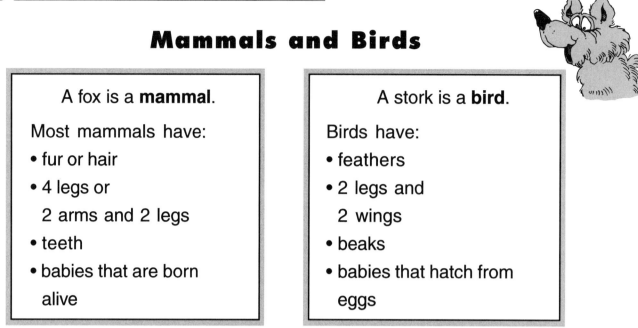

A fox is a **mammal**.	A stork is a **bird**.

Most mammals have:
• fur or hair
• 4 legs or
  2 arms and 2 legs
• teeth
• babies that are born
  alive
	Birds have:
	• feathers
	• 2 legs and
	  2 wings
	• beaks
	• babies that hatch from
	  eggs

Make a list of eight mammals and eight birds. Use the information on the charts to decide if an animal is a mammal or a bird.

Mammals	**Birds**
1. _____	1. _____
2. _____	2. _____
3. _____	3. _____
4. _____	4. _____
5. _____	5. _____
6. _____	6. _____
7. _____	7. _____
8. _____	8. _____

The Four Musicians

A German Folktale

An old donkey had grown weak and unable to work. When he learned that his owner was going to do away with him, the donkey ran away. "I will go to the city and become a musician," thought the donkey.

Along the way he met an old hound dog, a toothless old cat, and a rooster. They all had the same story to tell. They were too old to work and their owners were going to kill them. So each of the animals had run away. "Come with me to the city," said the donkey. "You can become musicians, too."

The four new friends walked along until it began to grow dark. The rooster flew to the top of a tree. He looked around to find some place for them to spend the night. "I see a light in an old building not far from here," said the rooster. "Let's see if we can stay there."

When they reached the building, the donkey peeked through a window. Inside were a gang of robbers sitting around a table covered with good things to eat. The gold they had stolen was scattered around the table, too.

"If we chase them away, we will have food and shelter," said the donkey. Very quietly, the donkey put his front feet on the window ledge. The other animals jumped up onto his back. The four friends started to sing. The donkey brayed, the hound dog howled, the cat screeched, and the rooster crowed.

Folktales & Fables • EMC 757

The noise was so horrible that the robbers nearly knocked each other over in their haste to run away.

The four friends ate the food that the robbers had left behind. Then they settled down for a good night's sleep. The donkey lay down on some straw in the front yard. The hound dog lay down by the front door. The cat lay down in front of the fireplace. And the rooster perched on a beam of the roof. Soon they were fast asleep.

After midnight the leader of the robbers sent a man to check out the house. If it was safe, they would go back to get their gold.

When the man peeked in, he didn't see the animals in the dark. Feeling braver, he went in the front door. He saw the old cat's eyes shining in the darkness. Thinking it was a monster, he ran screaming from the house. As he ran out of the house, he stepped on the dog, who bit him in the leg. As he ran across the yard, the donkey kicked him in the back. The man's screams woke up the rooster, who started to crow.

When the man got back to the forest, he told the robbers how horrible it had been. "A monster with eyes of fire lives in that building. Another monster stabbed me in my leg with a knife. Then a big black monster beat me with a wooden club. A little monster on the roof kept calling, 'Chuck him up to me!' I didn't think I was going to get away!"

The robbers agreed that no amount of gold was worth going back into that horrible place. The four friends were so happy and comfortable that they never went to the city. And they never became musicians.

Name _____

Questions about
The Four Musicians

1. List the four animal characters in *The Four Musicians*.

_____   _____

_____   _____

2. Why had the animals left their homes?

_____

3. How did the animals find a place to stay for the night?

_____

4. How did the animals scare the gang of robbers away?

_____

5. Why did the leader of the robbers send a man back to the house?

_____

6. Why did the old animals never go to the city?

_____

_____

Name _____

What Does It Mean?

Write each word after its meaning.

| beam | gang | perched | shelter |
| bray | ledge | scattered | worth |

1. a group of people going around together _____

2. threw around; sprinkled _____

3. a place that covers or protects from weather or danger _____

4. a loud noise made by a donkey _____

5. sat on _____

6. a narrow shelf _____

7. a large, long piece of timber or steel used in building _____

8. value; usefulness _____

What does the phrase **do away with** mean in this story?

_____

_____

What was the robber doing when he **checked out the building**?

_____

_____

Name _____

The Sounds of oo

Write each word under the correct sound.

g**oo**se	t**oo**k
_____ _____	_____ _____
_____ _____	_____ _____
_____ _____	_____ _____

roof	food	crook	tooth
cook	good	soon	too
rookie	wooden	rooster	cookie

● ● ● Contractions ● ● ●

Write the contractions for these words.

1. we will _____   5. I will   _____

2. he is _____   7. are not _____

3. will not _____   8. they have _____

4. it is _____   9. should not _____

In a contraction, what word do these letters replace?

1. 'll _____   3. n't _____

2. 's _____   4. 've _____

Name _____

Synonyms

Synonyms are words that have about the same meaning.
Match the synonyms.

1. place	began
2. peeked	location
3. started	looked
4. horrible	terrible

5. gang	also
6. old	tale
7. story	group
8. too	ancient

Replace each underlined word with its synonym.

1. There was a <u>terrible</u> accident at the fireworks factory. _____

2. An <u>ancient</u> woman worked in her flower garden. _____

3. Father told us an interesting <u>tale</u> about his grandfather. _____

••• They Go Together •••

Write a word to complete each comparison.

1. **dark** is to **night** as **light** is to ____day____

2. **juice** is to **drink** as **bread** is to _____

3. **A** is to **letters** as **9** is to _____

4. **fur** is to **cat** as **feather** is to _____

5. **paper** is to **tear** as **glass** is to _____

6. **mud** is to **dirty** as **soap** is to _____

The Shoemaker and the Elves

A German Folktale

Once upon a time there was a kindly shoemaker. Times were hard and he couldn't earn enough money to live on. All he had left was the leather for one pair of shoes. The shoemaker cut out the shoes and set them aside. He planned to sew them later.

At daybreak the shoemaker sat down at his workbench to sew the shoes. To his surprise, he saw a beautiful pair of shoes. They were perfect with tiny, neat stitches. The shoemaker called to his wife, "Come and see what I've found! Who could have done this?" His wife put the shoes in the window of the shop.

Soon a customer came into the shop. "How much are those beautiful shoes in the window?" asked the woman. "I must have them for my husband."

With the money from the sale of the shoes, the shoemaker bought leather to make two more pairs. Again the shoemaker cut out the shoes and left them on his workbench to finish the next day.

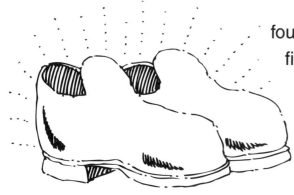

In the morning the shoemaker found that both pairs of shoes had been finished. His wife put the shoes in the shop's window. Soon both pairs of shoes had been sold for a high price. Before long the shoemaker and his wife were making a good living.

One evening the shoemaker said to his wife, "I'm going to wait up tonight to see who has been doing my work for me." His wife agreed to wait with him. That night the couple hid behind a curtain to see what would happen.

As the clock struck midnight, two tiny elves, barefooted and dressed in rags, appeared. The elves hopped up onto the workbench and quickly went to work. They sewed and tapped and polished shoes until daybreak. Then the elves left as quickly as they had come.

"Oh, my!" exclaimed the shoemaker's wife. "I have never seen such a sight in all my life. Those hard-working elves have made us rich. What can we do to thank them?"

"I will make them shoes," decided the shoemaker. "You can make them something to wear."

The shoemaker made each elf a pair of tiny shoes. His wife made each elf a shirt, a coat, and a pair of trousers. When the clothes were finished, the shoemaker laid them on the workbench. He and his wife hid behind the curtain to see what the little elves would do.

At midnight the elves hopped up onto the workbench as they did every night. When they saw the clothes lying there, the elves began to laugh. They dressed themselves in the twinkling of an eye. The elves danced out the door and down the street and were never seen again.

Folktales & Fables • EMC 757

Name _____

Questions about
The Shoemaker and the Elves

1. What was the shoemaker's problem?

_____

2. Every night the shoemaker left leather on his workbench. What did he find every morning?

_____

3. Who was doing all the work for the shoemaker?

_____

4. Why did the shoemaker and his wife make tiny clothes and shoes?

_____

5. Why were the shoemaker and his wife no longer poor?

_____

6. The elves never came back again after they got new clothes. Where do you think they went?

_____

_____

● ● ● Think About It ● ● ●

The elves helped the shoemaker and his wife. On another sheet of paper, list three ways you could help someone.

Name _____

What Does It Mean?

Write each word after its meaning. You will not use all of the words.

customer	elves	leather	stitches
curtain	evening	pair	trousers
earn	husband	perfect	wait

1. a pair of pants _____

2. a person who buys something _____

3. not spoiled in any way _____

4. material made from the skin of an animal _____

5. the time between sunset and bedtime _____

6. tiny beings; imaginary little people in stories _____

• • • Words with More Than One Meaning • • •

1. In the phrase **sold at a high price**, **high** means:

   ⃝ up above the ground   ⃝ a shrill voice   ⃝ expensive

2. In the phrase **all he had left**, **left** means:

   ⃝ one of your hands   ⃝ a direction   ⃝ the amount remaining

3. In the phrase **window of the shop**, **shop** means:

   ⃝ a place where things are sold   ⃝ to go and buy things

Name _____

Spell Long *a*

The sound of long **a** can be spelled many ways.

a–e   **ay**   **ai**   **ey**   **eigh**   **ea**

Circle the letters that spell long **a** in each of these words.

sale	steak	paint	break
they	crayon	eighty	wait
sleigh	make	came	day
player	prey	weight	

Fill in the missing letters to name the pictures.

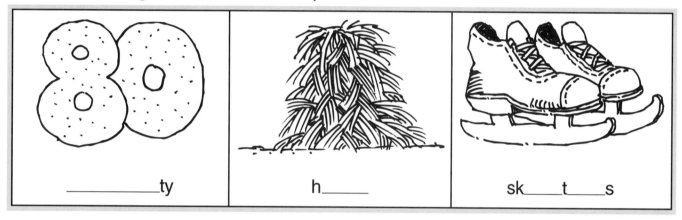

_____ty   h_____   sk____t____s

● ● ● Add a Suffix ● ● ●

A **suffix** comes at the end of a word to change it.

less–without   **ly**–in what manner   **ful**–filled with

Add the correct suffix to each word.

1. in a quick way   quick_____   5. in a kind way   kind_____

2. very pretty   beauti_____   6. able to help   help_____

3. in a happy way   happi_____   7. having no weight   weight_____

4. without a home   home_____   8. having no money   penni_____

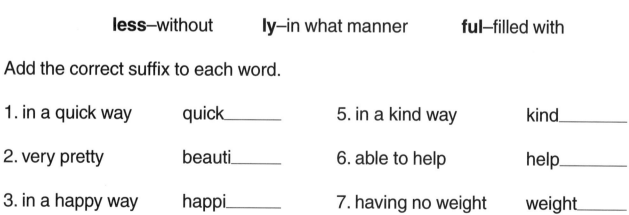

Name _____

Figures of Speech

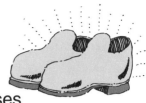

In the twinkling of an eye means **very fast**. Match the colorful phrases below to what they mean.

Stop bugging me!

It's raining cats and dogs.

She has a green thumb.

Lend a hand.

That's the way the
cookie crumbles.

You put your foot in
your mouth.

Stop pulling my leg.

I did it in two shakes
of a lamb's tail.

Help someone.

You said something
embarrassing or stupid.

The rain is very heavy.

Leave me alone.

Stop teasing me.

She's good at making
plants grow.

I did it very quickly.

That's just the way
something happens.

• • • Words for *Said* • • •

Find words in the story to complete these sentences.

1. The shoemaker _____, "Come and see what I've found!"

2. "How much are those beautiful shoes?" _____ the woman.

3. "Oh, my!" _____ the shoemaker's wife.

4. "I will make them shoes," _____ the shoemaker.

Name _____

An Interview

A reporter from a local newspaper is interviewing the shoemaker
and his wife. Write the answers you think they would give to the reporter's questions.

Reporter: "What did you think when you first saw the shoes that had been made for you?"

Shoemaker: _____

_____

Wife: _____

_____

Reporter: "How did your life change with the help given by the elves?

Shoemaker: _____

_____

Wife: _____

_____

Reporter: "What do you plan to do now that the elves have gone?"

Shoemaker: _____

_____

Wife: _____

_____

The Rabbit That Ran Away

A Fable from India

A nervous rabbit sat under a palm tree. A coconut fell to the ground behind her. When she heard the noise, she jumped up. "The Earth is breaking apart!" she thought. Without even looking to see what had made the noise, she started to run as fast as she could.

Another rabbit saw her running. He called out, "Why are you running, Miss Rabbit?"

"I don't have time to stop," said the rabbit. "The Earth is breaking apart, and I am running away!"

When the other rabbit heard this, he began to run, too. Each rabbit they met ran with them after hearing that the Earth was breaking apart. Soon hundreds of rabbits were running as fast as they could.

Then larger animals like deer and tigers began to join them. Each animal cried, "The Earth is breaking apart!" and ran as fast as it could.

A wise old lion saw the animals running and shouting. He ran in front of them and roared, "STOP!"

This stopped the animals. They knew they must obey the King of Beasts. "How do you know the Earth is breaking apart?" asked the lion.

The little rabbit stepped forward and said, "Oh, great king, I heard it."

"Where did you hear it?" asked the lion.

"I was resting under a palm tree. Then I heard the sound of the Earth breaking apart," said the little rabbit.

"Come and show me where this happened," said the lion.

"No, no," said the little rabbit, "I can't go near that tree. I'm too frightened."

"I will carry you on my back," said the lion. So the little rabbit went with the lion back to the palm tree. There they saw the big coconut lying under the tree.

"You silly rabbit," said the lion. "It was the sound of the coconut falling on the ground that you heard. The Earth is not breaking apart." The lion scolded the rabbit. "Be sure that what you are saying is true before you tell others."

Then the lion ran back and told the other animals what had really happened. The animals walked away whispering, "The Earth is not breaking apart."

If it hadn't been for the wise old lion, the animals might still be running.

Name _____

Questions about
The Rabbit That Ran Away

1. Why did the nervous rabbit start running?

   _____

2. Why did all of the other animals run after the rabbit?

   _____

3. Who stopped the animals? How did he do it?

   _____

   _____

4. How did the lion prove the Earth was not breaking apart?

   _____

5. What lesson did the animals learn?

   _____

6. What do you think the rabbit will do the next time she hears a loud noise? Why?

   _____

   _____

● ● ● Think About It ● ● ●

Write about a time you were frightened by a noise.

What did you hear?   _____

What did you do?   _____

Were you really in danger?   _____

Name _____

What Does It Mean?

Match each word to its meaning.

1. scold   to speak very softly

2. nervous   to do as you are told

3. whisper   sounds

4. noise   to speak sharply to; find fault with

5. coconut   have knowledge; make good choices

6. wise   easily excited or upset

7. obey   a hard brown fruit of a kind of palm tree

Draw:

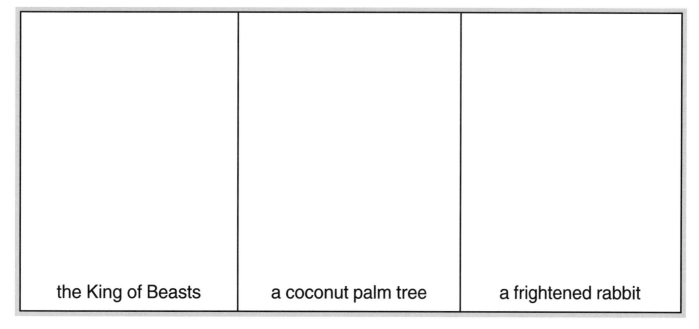

| the King of Beasts | a coconut palm tree | a frightened rabbit |

            Folktales & Fables • EMC 757

Name _____

What Says er?

Circle the letters that say **er** in each of these words.

her   world   earth   curse   bird

Use the letters you circled to fill in the blanks.

1. The animals h_____d that the w_____ld was breaking apart.

2. What oth_____ col_____ does this p_____se come in?

3. A n_____vous t_____key hid und_____ a bush.

4. The n_____se goes to w_____k _____ly in the morning.

5. The small_____ children were f_____st in line.

● ● ● How Many Syllables? ● ● ●

Find words in the story to complete this chart.

one-syllable words	two-syllable words	three-syllable words
_____	_____	_____
_____	_____	_____
_____	_____	_____
_____	_____	_____

Name _____

Cause and Effect

Write the effect of each cause.

Cause	Effect
A coconut fell from a tree and landed with a big noise behind a nervous rabbit.	_____ _____ _____

Cause	Effect
Larger animals saw hundreds of rabbits running away.	_____ _____ _____

Cause	Effect
The King of Beasts took the frightened rabbit back to the palm tree.	_____ _____ _____

Folktales & Fables • EMC 757

The Little People

A Native American Fable

Long ago, when my people lived close to nature, little people lived on the Earth. Even though they were small, they were very powerful.

This story tells what happened when my great-great-great-grandfather met two of the little people.

One day, when he was just seven, a little boy went hunting. He took his bow and arrows to shoot small birds. It was the way growing boys learned to hunt. It was their schooltime.

The little boy walked along the river, looking for water birds to shoot. Suddenly, he heard a sound on the water. He was surprised to see a tiny canoe coming down the river. In the canoe were four of the tiniest little men he had ever seen. They rowed the canoe right up to the boy and stopped.

The little men greeted the boy. Then one of the men asked, "Would you like to trade your bow and arrows with one of us?"

The boy didn't stop to think. He just said, "No, thank you. It would be silly to trade. Your bow and arrows are much smaller than mine."

One of the tiny men took his bow and shot an arrow straight up. The arrow disappeared into the sky. The boy watched and waited, but the arrow did not come back down. The little man said, "Remember what I say, small one. The biggest things are not always the best."

The little men stepped back into their canoe. They picked up their canoe paddles and set off down the river. They soon disappeared around a bend in the river.

The boy ran home moving as swiftly as a young deer. "Come quickly!" he shouted. "I have something to tell you."

His family gathered around to hear his tale. His parents frowned as he told the family what had happened. His grandfather scolded the boy. He said, "You made a big mistake not trading with the little people. One of their bows and arrows would have made you a mighty hunter. Bigger is not always better, my grandson."

That day my great-great-great-grandfather learned a lesson. It is a mistake to judge people by their size. You never know who or what they may really be.

This lesson has been handed down from father to son in my family ever since.

Name _____

Questions about
The Little People

1. Why was the little boy walking along the river?

_____

2. What surprised the boy?

_____

3. What did the little people want to do?

_____

4. Why wouldn't the boy trade with the little people?

_____

5. Why did his grandfather scold the boy?

_____

_____

6. What lesson did the boy learn?

_____

_____

● ● ● **Think About It** ● ● ●

The boy in the story needed to learn to be a good hunter when he grew up. Going to the river to practice hunting with a bow and arrows was like going to school for him.

On another sheet of paper, write about something you are learning at school that will help you when you grow up.

Name _____

What Does It Mean?

Match each word to its meaning.

1. trade	strong; mighty
2. powerful	a short oar used to row a boat or canoe
3. mistake	a light boat pointed at both ends
4. paddle	to move a boat or canoe using paddles or oars
5. judge	to make an exchange
6. canoe	very small
7. row	to decide; form an opinion
8. tiny	a misunderstanding; an error

Write the names of the pictures.

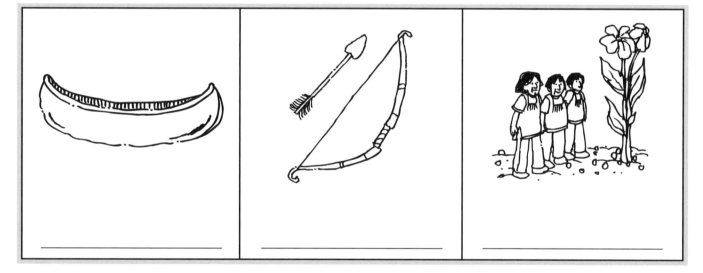

_____   _____   _____

• • • Synonyms • • •

Find three words in the story that mean about the same as **not very big**.

_____   _____   _____

Name _____

Spell Long Vowel Sounds

Circle the letter or letters in each word that make the long vowel sound.
Then write the sound on the line.

1. meat __e__   6. player _____   11. kind _____

2. smile _____   7. right _____   12. scream _____

3. coach _____   8. paint _____   13. use _____

4. greed _____   9. try _____   14. movie _____

5. follow _____   10. though _____   15. sleigh _____

• • • Homographs • • •

Homographs are words that are spelled the same. They may have the same or
different sounds. They do have different meanings.

bow and arrows   **bow** to the queen   **bow** in her hair

Write two sentences for each homograph. Use a different meaning in each sentence.

| bat |

1. _____

2. _____

| bark |

1. _____

2. _____

| close |

1. _____

2. _____

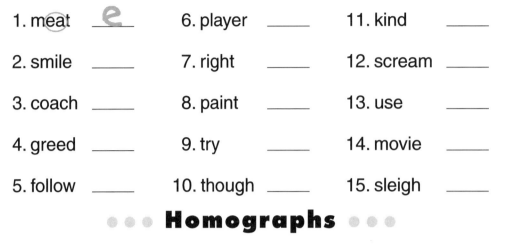

Name _____

Rhyming Words

Find the words in the story that rhyme with these words.

Final sounds spelled the same:	Final sounds **not** spelled the same:
know _____	heard _____
tall _____	bean _____
could _____	why _____
eleven _____	comb _____
strong _____	bough _____

● ● ● Adding Suffixes—*er, est* ● ● ●

Add **er** and **est** endings to these words.

	er	est
small	_____	_____
fast	_____	_____
big	_____	_____
tiny	_____	_____

Circle the correct word to complete each sentence.

1. That is the _____ girl I have ever seen.   happier   happiest

2. The male elephant is _____ than the female.   heavier   heaviest

3. My dad is _____ than my mother.   taller   tallest

4. Who is the _____ student in your school?   smarter   smartest

The Crow and the Peacock

A Folktale from China

Tiger was getting married and Peacock and Crow were invited to the wedding. At that time crows were as white as clouds and peacocks were as yellow as butter.

"I think we need to be more colorful for such an important wedding," said Peacock.

"That's an excellent idea," said Crow. "I know how we can do it. I can get paint in all the colors of the rainbow for us to use."

Crow went right to work painting Peacock. He was a great artist. He painted colorful designs and beautiful pictures all over Peacock's feathers. He made Peacock's tail the most beautiful of all.

When Crow was finished, Peacock looked at himself in a pool of water. "Oh! How beautiful I am! My tail looks like it is covered with precious gems," he exclaimed as he did a joyful dance.

 Folktales & Fables • EMC 757

Now it was Crow's turn. "Peacock, it is time for you to paint my feathers," said Crow.

But Peacock was so proud of how he looked, he didn't want anyone else to be as beautiful. He wasn't going to paint the crow's feathers.

Peacock said, "Crow, didn't you hear Eagle? Hurry! We must fly away from here. We are in danger." While he pretended to be in a hurry to escape, Peacock quickly knocked over the cans of paint. All but one can spilled into the pool of water.

"I didn't hear an eagle cry," said Crow.

"Then there is no danger," said Peacock. "Come here and I will paint you."

"But the paint has been spilled," pointed out Crow. "It's hopeless."

"There is one pot left," said Peacock. "Come here and I'll paint you with it. We must hurry. It's almost time for the wedding."

When Peacock was finished, Crow went to look at himself in the pool of water. The moment he saw himself, Crow began to complain. He was so angry he choked up and could only scream, "Caw! Caw!" at the proud peacock.

Ever since that time crows have been black with harsh voices. And peacocks have been beautiful with feathers in a rainbow of colors.

Name _____

Questions about
The Crow and the Peacock

1. What had Crow and Peacock been invited to?

_____

2. Why did Crow and Peacock think they needed to be more colorful?

_____

3. What was Crow's idea?

_____

4. Describe how Crow painted Peacock.

_____

5. Why didn't Peacock want to paint Crow?

_____

6. Why did Peacock pretend they were in danger?

_____

7. Describe how Peacock painted Crow.

_____

8. How do you think Crow felt about Peacock after what happened?

_____

●●● **Think About It** ●●●

On another sheet of paper, write about what makes a good friend.

Name _____

What Does It Mean?

Write each word after its meaning.

proud   harsh   designs   pool

artist   gems   moment   precious

1. a person who is a skilled painter, musician, or writer   _____

2. a small pond; a small body of still water   _____

3. rough to touch or unpleasant to hear   _____

4. patterns   _____

5. thinking too well of yourself   _____

6. a small amount of time; a minute   _____

7. very valuable; worth a lot   _____

8. jewels   _____

••• Birds •••

Circle the birds in this list. Then find the birds in the word search.

crow   jellyfish   pelican

chicken   eagle   turkey

octopus   owl   robin

goose   peacock   shark

swan   whale   wren

```
P E A C O C K W C
G H E O N H E R A
O O S W E I M E T
O P E L I C A N C
S O T U R K E Y R
E S W A N E Z D O
E A G L E N C O W
U P R O B I N G X
```

Name _____

The Sounds of *g*

Listen to the sound the letter **g** makes in the words below.
Write **g**, **j**, or **silent** on the lines.

1. tiger ____*g*____   5. edge _____   9. got _____

2. gems _____   6. gorilla _____   10. giraffe _____

3. sign _____   7. gather _____   11. guess _____

4. giant _____   8. right _____   12. genie _____

• • • Suffixes *less* and *ful* • • •

Write the base word and add the correct suffix.

less means **without**   **ful** means **full of**

1. without hope   _____
                         base word + suffix

2. filled with hope   _____
                         base word + suffix

3. filled with wonder   _____
                         base word + suffix

4. without harm   _____
                         base word + suffix

                   Folktales & Fables • EMC 757

Name _____

Similes

Similes are figures of speech that compare two things in an interesting way.

Match:

1. as yellow as   bee

2. as cold as   wink

3. as hard as a   mouse

4. as busy as a   butter

5. as quick as a   ice

6. as quiet as a   rock

Write your own similes.

1. as funny as _____   4. as round as _____

2. as soft as _____   5. as old as _____

3. as hot as _____   6. as slow as _____

● ● ● Divide Words into Syllables ● ● ●

A VCCV word is divided between the two consonants.

silly   sil–ly   into   in–to

Divide these words.

1. butter _____–_____   5. often _____–_____

2. tender _____–_____   6. funny _____–_____

3. only _____–_____   7. letter _____–_____

4. worry _____–_____   8. invite _____–_____

The Boy Who Cried Wolf

An Aesop Fable

A shepherd boy was in charge of tending a flock of sheep. Every morning he took the sheep to a meadow near his village. Every evening he brought the sheep back home. All day long he watched the sheep to make sure they were not harmed or didn't wander off and get lost.

One day the shepherd boy began to complain. "I am bored," he said. "There is nothing to do but watch these silly sheep eat grass. Nothing different ever happens." As he watched the sheep munching on the tall green grass, he had an idea. What fun it would be to fool the villagers. He would pretend that a wolf was attacking the flock of sheep.

"Wolf! Wolf!" he shouted. The villagers came running with pitchforks and clubs to drive off the wolf. When they arrived there was no wolf. There was just the naughty shepherd boy laughing his head off.

Again and again, the shepherd boy called wolf. Again and again the villagers came. Each time there was no wolf.

At last, one day, a hungry wolf crept up on the flock. When the shepherd boy saw the wolf, he began to shout, "Wolf! Wolf!" He shouted and shouted, but no one came. The villagers thought the boy was up to his old tricks, so they ignored his calls. The wolf killed sheep after sheep before the boy finally drove it away.

The shepherd boy finally learned that no one believes a liar even when he is telling the truth.

Name _____

Questions about
The Boy Who Cried Wolf

1. What was the shepherd boy's job?

   _____

2. Why was the shepherd boy bored?

   _____

3. What trick did he play on the villagers?

   _____

4. Why didn't the villagers come when a wolf really came to kill the sheep?

   _____

5. What lesson did the shepherd boy learn?

   _____

   _____

6. What do you think will happen to the shepherd boy? Why?

   _____

   _____

● ● ● Think About It ● ● ●

Why do you think people sometimes tell lies?

_____

_____

_____

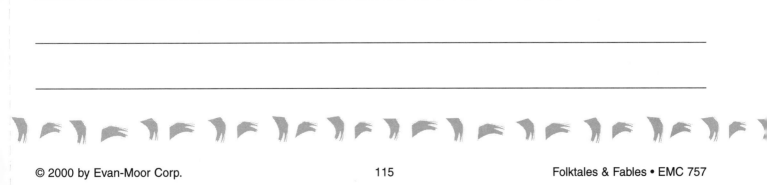

Name _____

What Does It Mean?

Write each word after its meaning.

shepherd	village	tend
pretend	flock	munch
ignore	wander off	liar

1. a very small town   _____

2. to make believe   _____

3. to pay no attention to   _____

4. a person who takes care of a flock of sheep   _____

5. a person who is not truthful   _____

6. to take care of   _____

7. to chew on something   _____

8. a group of animals of one kind herded together   _____

9. to move from here to there with no purpose   _____

● ● ● What Is It Called? ● ● ●

Write the correct name for each group of animals below.

gaggle	herd	flock
pod	school	swarm

1. a _____ of chickens   3. a _____ of whales

2. a _____ of fish

Name _____

Add a Prefix

A **prefix** comes in front of a word to change it.

Add the correct prefix to complete the words below.

un–not   **pre**–before   **under**–below

1. not happy   _____happy   4. before the game   _____game

2. below ground   _____ground   5. not comfortable   _____comfortable

3. see before   _____view   6. below the road   _____pass

Write a sentence using each new word you made.

1. _____

2. _____

3. _____

4. _____

5. _____

6. _____

••• What Doesn't Belong? •••

Make an **X** on the word in each group that does not belong.

village	state		yell	exclaim		eagle	kite
city	town		whisper	shout		jet	dog

Name _____

Same–Opposite

Circle the pairs of words that are opposites.

Make an **X** on the pairs of words that mean the same.

over–under   give–take   wee–small

full–empty   raced–hurried   front–back

large–big   deep–shallow   noisy–quiet

wept–cried   work–rest   leap–jump

••• Using Homophones •••

Circle the correct words.

1. Grandmother is going to teach me how to _____ clothes for my doll.
              sow   sew

2. While we were picking wild black_____ we saw a _____ cub.
          buries   berries   bear   bare

3. My _____ T-shirt has a picture of a _____ and a baby fawn.
      new   knew   dough   doe

4. He got a splinter in his _____ when he stepped on that old
          he'll   heel

_____.
bored   board

              Folktales & Fables • EMC 757

The Sun and the Wind

An Aesop Fable

The sun and the wind were having an argument. Each claimed to be the strongest. "We should have a contest to see who is stronger," said the sun.

Just then they saw a traveler strolling down a dusty country road. "I know what we can do," said the wind. "Let's see which of us can make the traveler take off his coat."

They agreed to take turns, and the winner would be declared the strongest.

The wind went first, blowing as hard as it could. The traveler buttoned his coat and turned up the collar around his neck. Harder and harder blew the wind, trying to blow off the traveler's coat. But the harder he blew, the tighter the traveler held on to his coat. After half an hour, the wind had to give up.

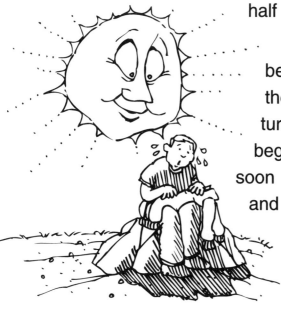

Now it was the sun's turn. The sun beamed down upon the traveler. Soon the traveler unbuttoned his coat and turned down his collar. Then the sun began to shine even brighter. The man soon found it too hot to walk. He stopped and pulled off his coat. The traveler sat down on a large boulder under a shade tree to cool off.

In only a few minutes the sun had won the contest.

119

Name _____

Questions about
The Sun *and the* Wind

1. What were the sun and the wind arguing about?

   _____

2. How were they going to decide which of them was stronger?

   _____

3. What did they each do to try to win?

   the wind: _____

   the sun: _____

4. What finally made the traveler take off his coat?

   _____

5. What do you think? Is the sun stronger than the wind? Explain your answer.

   _____

   _____

   _____

6. Which lesson did the wind learn?
   a. Blowing harder would prove the wind was strongest.
   b. Force isn't always the best way to win.

● ● ● Think About It ● ● ●

On another sheet of paper, think of another way to get someone to remove his or
her coat.

Name _____

What Does It Mean?

Replace the underlined words with words from the story.

1. The sun and the wind were having a <u>disagreement</u>. _____

2. A man was <u>walking</u> down the road. _____

3. It took only a few <u>moments</u>. _____

4. The sun <u>shone</u> down on the traveler. _____

5. The winner would be <u>named</u> the strongest. _____

6. They saw a <u>hiker</u> walking down the road. _____

7. He laid his coat on a large <u>rock</u>. _____

● ● ● Synonyms ● ● ●

Match the words that have about the same meanings.

1. huge	plan
2. beam	unsafe
3. angry	gigantic
4. powerful	stay
5. design	close
6. dangerous	mad
7. remain	strong
8. near	shine

121   Folktales & Fables • EMC 757

The Sounds of *ou*

Listen to the vowel sound in each word. Write the letters and symbols to show the sound made by **ou**.

our–**ow**	sh**ou**lder–**ō**	w**ou**ld–**ŏŏ**
b**ou**ght–**aw**	y**ou**–**o͞o**	c**ou**ple–**ŭ**

1. hour _____

2. boulder _____

3. should _____

4. thought _____

5. your _____

6. country _____

7. shout _____

8. double _____

9. tour _____

10. could _____

11. cough _____

12. though _____

13. count _____

14. young _____

● ● ● Articles ● ● ●

The articles **a** and **an** come before a noun.
A is used before words starting with a consonant sound.
An is used before words starting with a vowel sound.

_a_ traveler

_____ argument

_____ coat

_____ old man

_____ boulder

_____ hour

_____ road

_____ elephant

_____ inn

_____ uncle

_____ shade tree

_____ contest

Name _____

Cause and Effect

Write the cause for each effect.

Cause	Effect
_____ _____ _____	The traveler buttoned his coat and turned up his collar.
_____ _____ _____	The traveler took off his coat and sat down under a shade tree.

● ● ● Arguments ● ● ●

Write about a time you had an argument with someone. What did you argue about?

_____

_____

_____

How did you settle the argument?

_____

_____

_____

How the Princess Learned to Laugh
A Folktale from Poland

There once was a princess who never laughed. Her father, the king, was worried about his daughter. He promised her hand in marriage to any young man who could make her laugh.

A king in a nearby country had two sons. He thought that his elder son was clever, but that his younger son was a fool. Each of his sons wanted to try to make the princess laugh so he could marry her.

The elder son, who was proud and selfish, took a court jester's rattle and cap and set off on his journey. He was sure he would make the princess laugh and would then marry her.

The prince stopped to eat his midday meal near a well. An old man came up to the prince. He asked, "Can you spare a little bread for a hungry traveler?" The selfish prince chased the old man away with his horsewhip.

When the prince arrived at the castle, he put on the jester's cap and stood before the princess. He shook the rattle, did a little dance, and made funny faces. She didn't smile. He told jokes. She didn't smile. He turned cartwheels and stood on his head. Nothing he did made the princess even crack a smile. He had to return home a failure.

When the younger son heard that his brother had failed, he set off to try. He too met the old man when he stopped at the well to eat his midday meal. When the old man ask for some bread, the kind prince gladly shared what he had.

"Bless you, friend!" the old man said. They ate their meal together, then the young prince settled down to take a nap.

While he slept, the young prince had a strange dream. In his dream the old man was an angel sent to Earth to find someone kind. When the prince awoke, he saw a strange sight. There stood a golden coach shaped like a pumpkin. The coach was pulled by a goose and a gander. The coachman was a cross-eyed dog.

The young prince climbed into the coach and started off to the castle. Along the way people pointed and laughed at the strange coach. It was too late to go to the castle that day, so the young prince stopped at an inn, leaving the coach in the inn's courtyard.

The next morning, the innkeeper's greedy wife came into the courtyard. She began to cut gold off the coach with a large kitchen knife. "Oh, no!" she cried. "I'm stuck to the coach." She pulled and pulled, but she couldn't get free.

The young prince didn't see her as he got into the coach. Off he went to the castle, with the innkeeper's wife running along behind. Along the way people tried to pull her off the coach, but they got stuck, too. Soon,

the innkeeper's wife was stuck to the coach,

a baker was stuck to the innkeeper's wife,

a washerwoman was stuck to the baker, and

a soldier was stuck to the washerwoman.

As the coach reached the castle, people crowded around laughing at the ridiculous parade running behind.

The princess came to see what all the noise was about. Suddenly, the crowd heard a sound they had never heard before. It was the princess laughing harder than anyone! The next day the princess and the kind prince were married. And the princess was never sad again.

Name _____

Questions about

How the Princess Learned to Laugh

1. Why was the king worried about his daughter?

_____

2. What did the king promise any young man who could make his daughter laugh?

_____

3. Another king had two sons who wanted to try to make her laugh. Describe them.

   elder son: _____

   younger son: _____

4. How did the elder son try to make the princess laugh?

_____

_____

5. Who was the angel in the story? How did he repay the younger son for his kindness?

_____

_____

6. What finally made the princess laugh?

_____

_____

●●● Think About It ●●●

On another sheet of paper, write about how you would make the princess laugh.

Name _____

What Does It Mean?

Find words in the story to complete the following tasks.

1. Find two words that mean **wanting more than your share**.

   _____   _____

2. Find the character that:

   a. did tricks and told jokes   _____

   b. helped her husband run the inn   _____

   c. helped protect the country   _____

   d. was the ruler of the country   _____

3. Find the word that means:

   a. silly or laughable   _____

   b. a place for travelers to rest and get food   _____

   c. a toy that makes a noise when you shake it   _____

   d. close   _____

4. Match the phrases to their meanings.

   a. give a hand in marriage   begin to smile

   b. set off   allow to marry

   c. bless you   agree to do something

   d. crack a smile   start on a journey

   e. make a promise   may good things happen to you

Name _____

The Sounds of *gh*

The letters **gh** can be pronounced like the letter **f**.

They can also be **silent**.

Mark what you hear in these words.

rough	(f)	silent	**bought**	f	silent
laugh	f	silent	**tough**	f	silent
right	f	silent	**cough**	f	silent
thought	f	silent	**daughter**	f	silent

● ● ● The Sounds of *c* ● ● ●

Write the sound **c** makes in the following words.

cereal–**s**   **c**ount–**k**

1. magic _____   6. princess _____

2. face _____   7. court _____

3. coal _____   8. dance _____

4. castle _____   9. cent _____

5. once _____   10. cap _____

Decide which letter to use for the sound **s** in these words.

1. _____heep   4. _____enter

2. _____ity   5. _____ister

3. _____illy   6. pen_____il

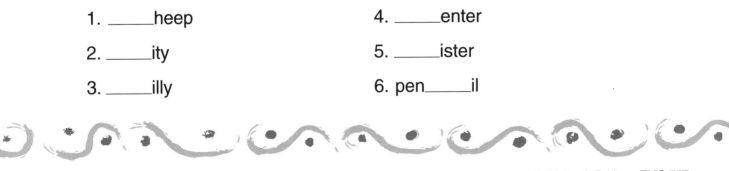

                     Folktales & Fables • EMC 757

Name _____

The Princes

Write about a time when the younger prince was:

1. surprised _____

_____

2. kind _____

_____

Write about a time when the elder prince was:

1. unkind _____

_____

2. disappointed _____

_____

● ● ● Past and Present ● ● ●

The words below are in the **present tense**. The words tell what happens now.
Write the past tense of each word to tell what already happened.

1. sleep _____ 5. stop _____

2. laugh _____ 6. arrive _____

3. think _____ 7. marry _____

4. shake _____ 8. come _____

   Folktales & Fables • EMC 757

Name _____

Write a Letter

Pretend you are the young prince. Write a letter to your father, the king, telling about what happened on your journey.

Dear Father,

Love,
Your Son

 Folktales & Fables • EMC 757

The Tiger and the Big Wind

A Folktale from Africa

Long, long ago there was a time when the rains had not come for a whole year. Without much food and water, all of the animals had become very hungry and very thirsty.

In all the hot, dry land there was one place where underground water had kept a large fruit tree alive. The juicy fruit was just waiting to be eaten. Why didn't the animals eat the fruit, you ask? A large tiger was resting under the tree.

Tiger was mean and selfish. He sat in the shade of the tree all day growling whenever any other animal came near. Tiger would say, "Stay away from my tree or I'll eat you up!"

One day a rabbit heard the animals of the forest talking about what was happening. "Oh, Wise Rabbit, what are we to do?" the animals asked.

Wise Rabbit thought about this for several days. Finally he called the animals together and said, "Listen and I will tell you what to do."

Early the next morning, while Tiger was still sleeping, the animals hid in the forest near the field where the fruit tree grew. The animals that lived on the ground stood near big, hollow logs. The animals that lived in the trees sat in the branches. The animals waited patiently for Wise Rabbit to arrive.

When Rabbit came, he was carrying a large rope. Rabbit ran across the field shouting, "Oh, my! Oh, my!"

The noise woke Tiger and he growled, "Stop making that horrible noise, Rabbit. I am sleeping!"

"Run, Tiger, run! A big wind is coming. It will blow everyone off the Earth!" As Rabbit said this, all the animals hiding in the forest began to make a loud racket.

The birds began to flap their wings, causing the leaves in the trees to shake about. The large animals began to beat on the hollow logs, making a terrible racket. Other animals ran around in the brush, until the whole forest seemed to be swaying in a terrible wind.

Tiger was terrified! "What should I do?" he screamed.

"You must run and try to find a safe place," said Wise Rabbit. "I can't help you now. I have to tie down the small animals with this rope or they will be blown off the Earth."

"You must tie me down first!" demanded Tiger.

Wise Rabbit shook his head, "You are strong enough to take care of yourself. I must help the smaller animals."

Tiger roared. "You must tie me up now or I will eat you!"

"Very well," said Wise Rabbit. "I will tie you up first." He tied Tiger tightly to the tree. When he was done, the rabbit called for the other animals to come out of the forest.

"Look at this greedy tiger," said Wise Rabbit. "He wanted to keep all of the fruit for himself instead of sharing with us. He forgot that food was put on the Earth for all to enjoy."

The selfish tiger could only watch as the animals sat together in the shade of the tree and feasted on the delicious fruit.

Folktales & Fables • EMC 757

Name _____

1. What had happened to make the animals hungry and thirsty?

   _____

2. How was the one fruit tree able to stay alive?

   _____

3. Why did the animals think the tiger was mean and selfish?

   _____

4. Wise Rabbit had a plan.

   a. What did he have the birds do?

   _____

   b. What did he have the large animals do?

   _____

   c. What made the brush move about?

   _____

   d. How did he manage to tie the tiger to the tree?

   _____

5. What had the selfish tiger forgotten about?

   _____

● ● ● Think About It ● ● ●

On another sheet of paper, write about how the animals in this story act like people.

Name _____

What Does It Mean?

Match each word to its meaning.

1. whole   more than two or three, but not many

2. several   empty inside; not solid

3. hollow   a place out of the sun

4. arrived   all of something

5. racket   noise

6. brush   came to a place

7. shade   tasty

8. delicious   shrubs, bushes, and small trees

Find words in the story to complete these sentences.

1. "May I have a drink?" asked the boy. "I'm very _____."

2. A _____ is 365 days long.

3. There are many different kinds of trees in the _____.

4. That stew has a _____ taste.

5. The _____ tiger wouldn't share the ripe _____.

Name _____

A Word Family—*eat*

Add **eat** to make new words.

b_____   s_____   wh_____

m_____   ch_____   tr_____

Write each new word above after its meaning.

1. a piece of furniture   _____

2. to pound on something   _____

3. a kind of grain   _____

4. animal flesh used for food   _____

5. to be dishonest   _____

6. something special to do or to eat   _____

● ● ● Contractions ● ● ●

The contractions **you're**, **it's**, and **they're** can be confused with other words.

Circle the correct word to complete each sentence.

1. What is _____ favorite food?   your   you're

2. _____ invited to my party.   Your   You're

3. "_____ too early for bed," said Anna.   Its   It's

4. Your dog is cute. What is _____ name?   its   it's

5. The firemen parked _____ truck by the fire hydrant.   their   they're

6. Next week _____ going on vacation.   their   they're

Name _____

Who Said It?

Match the characters to what they said.

• "Stay away from my tree!"

• "Listen and I'll tell you what to do."

• "Oh, my! Oh, my!"

• "You must tie me down first!"

• "A big wind is coming."

• "What should I do?"

●●● Words for *Said* ●●●

Complete these sentences that use different words for **said**.

1. "_____," screamed _____.

what was said   who said it

2. "_____," roared _____.

what was said   who said it

3. "_____," demanded _____.

what was said   who said it

4. "_____," growled _____.

what was said   who said it

Answer Key

Page 6
1. The old man and his wife lived on a small hill near the sea. OR The old man and his wife lived in a small shack with a crooked roof.
2. The old man caught fish in a net.
3. a. It could talk.
   b. It was magical. OR It could grant wishes.
4. The old woman wanted a loaf of bread.
5. The old woman wanted to rule the land and the sea and everything that lived there.
6. The golden fish took everything away because the wife was greedy. OR The golden fish took everything away because the wife wanted too much.

Answers will vary, but could include:
He was poor. He was a fisherman. He lived near the sea. He was kind to the golden fish. He did what his wife asked him to do.

Page 7
1. shack   5. grant
2. sea   6. loaf
3. shiny   7. washtub
4. begged   8. poor

1. loaf of bread — in the fishing net
2. shiny, golden fish — inside the old shack
3. wife dressed in rags — on a small hill near the sea
4. old shack — on the table

Page 8
1. a loaf of bread
2. a new washtub
3. a new house
4. to be rich
5. to be queen
6. to rule the land and sea and everything that lived there

Page 9

Long **i** Words		Short **i** Words	
kind	my	lived	rich
shiny	wife	into	will
find	why	wish	fish
tiny	time	give	his

Answers will vary, but could include:
1. fish, dish   6. pool, fool, tool
2. bill, hill, fill 7. gold, sold, told
3. band, hand, sand 8. pay, day, say
4. can, ran, fan   9. cut, nut, hut
5. pet, wet, bet

Page 10
(shiny) shack (golden) talking
bread (poor) table catch
(old) (greedy) (angry) (kind)

1. kind, old man OR poor, old man
2. shiny, golden fish

rich — less
new — poor
more — near
front — old
far — back

up — happy
funny — down
upset — outside
take — sad
inside — give

Page 12
1. The farmer and his wife wanted a goose to eat the weeds in their garden.
2. The farmer and his wife sold the golden eggs.
3. The farmer thought he would find a lot of golden eggs if he cut open the goose.
4. The goose had insides like all geese.
5. They learned not to be greedy.

1. (smile)   3. (smile)   5. (smile)
2. (frown)   4. (smile)   6. (frown)

Page 13
1. wife — a married woman
2. fair — a place to buy and sell farm products and animals
3. weeds — wild plants growing where they are not wanted
4. plump — round and full; a little bit fat
5. strange — unusual; not seen before
6. greedy — wanting more than your share

farmer	goose	egg
lucky	large	heavy
greedy	plump	golden
rich	magical	yellow

Page 14
3
5
2
4
1
6

Page 15
(they) mouth (that) think (their)
thin (this) with (another)

1. with   4. think
2. They   5. another
3. mouth

1. eggs   1. dishes   1. geese
2. nests   2. boxes   2. teeth
3. dogs   3. wishes   3. men
4. hats   4. brushes   4. mice

Page 16
Pictures will vary, but must show a goose sitting on a large golden egg in a nest.

Page 18
1. The cat was catching and eating the mice.
2. The mice met to think of how to stop the cat.
3. The little mouse said the mice should put a bell on the cat.
4. The bell would let the mice hear the cat coming so they could run away.
5. All of the mice left the room. None of them wanted to put the bell on the cat.
6. a. A plan isn't any good if it can't work.

Answers will vary.

Page 19
1. meeting
2. escape OR run for cover
3. run for cover OR escape
4. bell the cat
5. terrible
6. sneak

Page 20
1. eating
2. meeting
3. she
4. sneak

taller   tall<u>est</u>
old<u>er</u>   old<u>est</u>
young<u>er</u>   young<u>est</u>

1. old<u>est</u>   4. young<u>er</u>
2. old<u>er</u>   5. tall<u>er</u>
3. young<u>est</u>

Page 21

mouse room hungry quiet
shout   bell   neck   cookie
hooray old   cat   escape
mice   book little   hole

1. A hungry <u>cat</u> chased a little gray <u>mouse</u>.
2. The students hurried to their class<u>room</u> when the <u>bell</u> rang.
3. What kind of <u>cookie</u> do you like for dessert?

Page 22

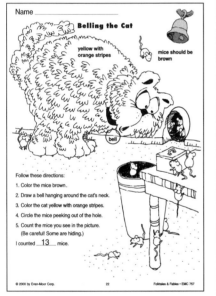

Page 25

1. Eagle wanted to see if Tortoise was really kind to his guests.
2. Tortoise fed Eagle tasty food. OR Tortoise fed Eagle as much food as Eagle wanted.
3. Eagle never invited Tortoise to his home to eat.
4. Tortoise hid in a gourd of food he gave to Eagle to take home.
5. a. He tried to peck Tortoise's shell.
   b. He tried to drop Tortoise to the ground from high in the sky.
6. Tortoise held on to Eagle's leg and wouldn't let go until Eagle took him home.

Answers will vary, but should include:
Tortoise learned that Eagle was unkind and selfish.
Eagle learned that Tortoise was kind and brave.

Page 26

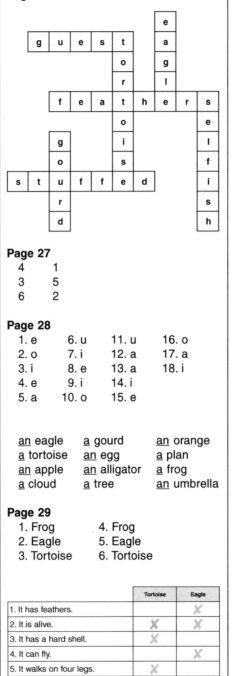

Page 27

4   1
3   5
6   2

Page 28

1. e	6. u	11. u	16. o
2. o	7. i	12. a	17. a
3. i	8. e	13. a	18. i
4. e	9. i	14. i	
5. a	10. o	15. e	

an eagle   a gourd   an orange
a tortoise   an egg   a plan
an apple   an alligator a frog
a cloud   a tree   an umbrella

Page 29

1. Frog   4. Frog
2. Eagle   5. Eagle
3. Tortoise 6. Tortoise

	Tortoise	Eagle
1. It has feathers.		X
2. It is alive.	X	X
3. It has a hard shell.	X	
4. It can fly.		X
5. It walks on four legs.	X	
6. It lives on land.	X	
7. It must eat to stay alive.	X	X
8. It has a strong beak and sharp claws.		X

Page 32

1. The farm wife had to make a large pancake because she had seven hungry children.
2. dear, sweet, nice, pretty, good, kind
3. The pancake rolled from place to place.
4. a hen, a duck, a pig
5. The pancake ran away because everyone wanted to eat it.
6. Piggy Wiggy said he would take the pancake across the brook. When the pancake jumped onto his snout, Piggy Wiggy ate the pancake.

A mother can cook a pancake.
Children do beg for a bite to eat.
~~A pancake can jump off a griddle.~~
~~A hen can talk like a person.~~
A pig can eat a pancake.
~~A pancake can roll down the road.~~
Children can run after their mother.
~~A pancake can jump onto the snout of a pig.~~

Page 33

griddle — a flat pan used for cooking
beg — to ask for something
hungry — needing food
snout — front part of a pig's head
clever — smart or skillful
brook — a little stream of water
quick as a wink — in a big hurry

1. she   4. they
2. her   5. them
3. it   6. me

Page 34

• Picture of the pancake jumping out of the pan, rolling out the door, or rolling down the road.

• Picture of one of the characters from the story chasing the pancake.

- Picture of Piggy Wiggy eating the pancake or rubbing his full stomach.

Page 35

a	e	i
fast	smell	griddle
had	hen	will
ran	end	wink
stamp	beg	quick
that	rest	give

o	u
hopped	stuck
stop	run
on	but
block	duck
not	such

rain — boy   rainbow
butter — bow   butterfly
pea — nut   peanut
cow — fly   butterfly

Page 36

Page 39
1. The days were warm and bright.
2. The grasshopper played and sang all day. OR
   The grasshopper hopped around and sang all day.
3. The ants carried seeds to their nest.
4. The ants were storing food to eat during the winter.
5. The grasshopper didn't have any food to eat.
6. The grasshopper learned that he should have stored some of his food in the summer to eat in the winter.
7. Answers will vary.

Answers will vary.

Page 40
1. summer winter
2. plenty
3. insects
4. bright
5. save store
6. field
7. busy
8. warm

summer — day
work — short
ask — play
stay — winter
night — go
tall — answer

sad — over
awake — small
under — early
late — happy
now — asleep
large — then

Page 41
grin   drain
grain   drive
gray   drop
ground   drummer
gravy   dream

back   black
sack   shack
tack   stack
crack   attack

1. shack
2. tack
3. crack
4. black
5. sack
6. back

Page 42
1. worked   working
2. played   playing

1. drummed   drumming
2. stopped   stopping

1. carried
2. cried

3	1	3
1	3	1
2	1	2
2	2	1

Page 43

Answers will vary, but should include some of the following:

Same—both are insects; both have six legs; both have antennae; both have three body parts

Different—ants crawl and grasshoppers hop and fly; ants are small and grasshoppers are big

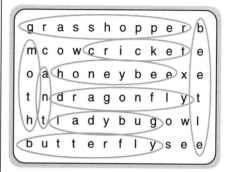

Page 46
1. The princess's favorite toy was a golden ball.
2. The ball fell into a deep well.
3. The frog wanted to go home with the princess and be her best friend.
4. The king made the princess take good care of the frog.
5. The frog turned into a prince. OR The magic spell was broken.
6. The princess kept her promise to the frog.
7. Answers will vary.

1. King—He was happy because the princess had learned to keep her promises.
2. Princess—She was happy because she didn't have to eat and sleep with a frog anymore.
3. Prince—He was happy because he wasn't a frog anymore.

Page 47

1. daughter — a girl child in a family
2. favorite — liked the most
3. weeping — crying
4. well — a deep hole in the ground containing water
5. promise — to give your word; agree to do something
6. complain — to say that something is wrong; to find fault
7. obey — to do as you are told
8. frown — an unhappy or angry look
9. remain — to stay where you are

youngest
slimy
favorite
unkind
large
golden

Page 48

knee   knight   knife

1. knock   4. sigh   7. talk
2. comb   5. listen 8. wrote
3. knew   6. wring   9. kneel

1. The princess saw an ugly frog by the well.
2. The king gave a golden ball to his daughter.
3. The princess didn't keep her promise.
4. The frog began to call, "Stop! Stop!" as the princess ran away.

Page 49

4
2
1
5
3

Page 50

Cause—The princess's ball fell into the well.
Effect—The frog got the ball out of the well.
Cause—The princess kept her promise to the frog.

Page 53

1. a. in the river
   b. in a tree by the riverbank
2. The crocodile mother wanted to eat the heart of a monkey.
3. The crocodile son told the monkey he would take him to get ripe fruit on the island. Then the crocodile planned to drown the monkey.
4. The monkey told the crocodile he had left his heart back home. When the crocodile took him back, the monkey climbed back into his tree.
5. Answers will vary.

Page 54

1. island   3. fruit
2. center   4. surface
   halfway   5. drown

1. to look at carefully
2. to be able to

Page 55

2
4
1
7
5
3
6

Page 56

1. e   5. e
2. i   6. i
3. e   7. i
4. i   8. e

At the end of many one-syllable words **y** says i.
At the end of many two-syllable words **y** says e.

1. sun   5. some
2. knew   6. prey
3. wood   7. fleas
4. two   8. hour

Page 57

	🐵	🐊
1. It is an animal.	X	X
2. It is covered in fur.	X	
3. I has thick, scaly skin.		X
4. It lives in trees.	X	
5. It spends most of the time in water.		X
6. It uses sharp teeth and strong jaws to catch prey.		X
7. It breathes air.	X	X
8. It eats mostly plants.	X	
9. It uses its strong tail to help it swim.		X
10. It lays eggs.		X
11. Its babies are born alive.	X	
12. It has humanlike eyes and ears.	X	

Page 59

1. Crow needed to find water.
2. in the creek bed
   in the pond
   in the horse's trough
   in the pitcher
3. The neck of the pitcher was too small for Crow to put her head in.
4. The pitcher was too heavy to tip over.
5. The water rose to the brim of the pitcher.
6. She got the idea when she saw a pile of pebbles in the garden.

Answers will vary.

Page 60

1. peered   3. brim   5. creek
2. swooped   4. idea   6. pebbles

1. b
2. c
3. a

Page 61

These words should be circled:
1. stone   4. oval   7. comb
2. no   5. sew   8. globe
3. toast   6. crow

fought   bought
sought   brought

1. brought   3. sought
2. fought   4. bought

Page 62

dropped   thought
flew   saw
began   gave
moaned   ate

1. flew   3. thought
2. ate   4. gave

1. swoop   6. slow
2. cry   7. raise
3. waste   8. drop
4. chase   9. hope
5. notice   10. hurry

Page 63

Character—Crow

Problem—Crow was thirsty. The only water she could find was in a pitcher with a narrow neck. She couldn't reach the water.

Solution—Crow saw a pile of pebbles. This gave her the idea to drop pebbles into the pitcher. The water rose up to the brim and then she could drink it.

Answers will vary.

Page 66
1. The old man and the old woman found the boy in a peach. OR The boy jumped out of a peach.
2. The ogres stole things from the villagers.
3. sword—to fight the ogres dumplings—to eat and give to the animals who helped him
4. dog—The dog bit the ogres' heels. monkey—The monkey jumped on the ogres' backs. bird—The bird pecked the ogres' heads.
5. Answers will vary, but could include: brave, clever, strong, a good son

Answers will vary, but could include:
1. worried, upset, frightened
2. happy, excited, relieved

Page 67
An ugly, old ogre complained, "I am so hungry I can hear my stomach rumble. I would like a dumpling like my mother used to make."

The ogre set off on a journey to find someone to make him a dumpling. He traveled many miles before coming to a house. When he knocked, a plump little lady opened the door and smiled kindly.

"I'm so hungry my stomach is

rumbling. I need a dumpling," explained the ogre. The little lady invited him in and began to cook. She made a huge, tasty dumpling.

The ogre cleaned his plate and, with a big smile on his ugly face, said, "Thanks, Mom!"

Page 68
1. A little boy jumped out of the peach.
2. The ogres started to steal from the villagers.
3. Momotaro gave the dog a dumpling and asked it to help him fight the ogres.
4. The other ogres begged for mercy.
5. His parents wept for joy when he came home.

Page 69

ed	d	t
waited	followed	jumped
headed	joined	pecked
shouted	begged	crossed
wanted	pinned	leaped

1. beach
2. teach
3. reach
4. peach
5. preach

Page 70

bites   takes   watches
chases   pushes   washes
weeps   breaks   wishes
grows   steals   returns

1. returns   4. pushes   7. grows
2. chases   5. breaks   8. washes
3. takes   6. watches

1. worries   4. tries
2. cries   5. hurries
3. carries   6. buries

Page 73
1. The boy wanted to get back the flour the North Wind had blown away.
2. cloth—The cloth became covered with good things to eat. ram—Gold coins fell out of the ram's mouth. stick—The stick would beat things and protect him.
3. The innkeeper had taken the magic cloth and the ram and left ordinary ones.

4. The boy pretended to be asleep. When the innkeeper tried to take the stick, the boy said the magic words. The stick beat the innkeeper until he gave back the magic cloth and the ram.
5. He learned not to steal from other people.

Answers will vary.

Page 74

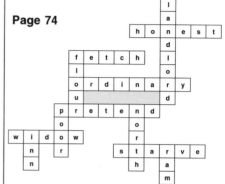

Page 75

ow		ō	
flower	tower	widow	own
town	clown	show	blow

1. storehouse   3. tablecloth
2. landlord   4. nightmare

Sentences will vary.

Page 76
1. whole   4. flower   7. in
2. peace   5. burro   8. beet
3. would   6. chews   9. dough

1. The gopher dug a **whole** in my garden. hole
2. Do you know how to make pizza **doe**? dough
3. The little **burrow** brayed, "Hee, haw!" burro

1. As the boy came out of the storehouse, the North Wind blew the flour away.
2. As the boy slept, the landlord crept into his room.
3. When the boy reached home, he showed the ram to his mother.
4. The boy lay down on the bed and pretended to be asleep.

Page 77
Pictures will vary, but must illustrate what is being said.

 Folktales & Fables • EMC 757

Page 79

1. Fox served the soup in a shallow dish so Stork couldn't eat any.
2. Answers will vary, but could include: Stork felt upset. Stork felt angry. Stork felt unhappy. Stork felt hungry.
3. Stork wanted to get even with Fox. OR
   Stork wanted to show Fox how it felt to have a trick played on him.
4. Stork put the stew in a tall, narrow jar so Fox couldn't eat it.
5. Answers should express in some way that it is not nice to play tricks on your friends.

Answers will vary.

Page 80

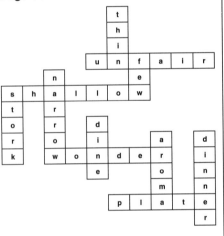

Page 81

soup who   blue few
stew fruit you   clue
soon knew two   suit

soup   fruit   two

unfair   unkind   uncomfortable

Page 82

Answers will vary, but must all be either a mammal or a bird.

Page 85

1. old donkey, toothless old cat, hound dog, rooster
2. The animals were old and couldn't work anymore so their owners were going to kill them.
3. The rooster flew to the top of a tree and saw an old building.

4. The animals made such a terrible noise when they sang that the robbers were frightened away.
5. The leader sent a man back to see if it was safe to return for the gold.
6. They were too comfortable where they were.

Page 86

1. gang
2. scattered
3. shelter
4. bray
5. perched
6. ledge
7. beam
8. worth

do away with—kill
checked out the building—looked to see if it was safe

Page 87

goose   took
roof   rooster   cook   rookie
food   tooth   crook good
soon   too   cookie wooden

1. we'll
2. he's
3. won't
4. it's
5. perched
6. shouldn't
7. I'll
8. aren't
9. they've

1. will   3. not
2. is   4. have

Page 88

1. place — location
2. peeked — looked
3. started — began
4. horrible — terrible
5. gang — group
6. old — ancient
7. story — tale
8. too — also

1. horrible
2. old
3. story

1. day   4. bird
2. eat   5. break
3. numbers   6. clean

Page 91

1. The shoemaker couldn't earn enough money to live on.
2. The shoemaker found beautiful new shoes.
3. Two tiny elves were doing all the work.
4. They made tiny clothes and shoes because the elves were dressed in rags and had no shoes. OR They made tiny clothes and shoes to thank the elves for helping them.
5. The shoemaker and his wife sold the shoes the elves made for a lot of money.
6. Answers will vary.

Answers will vary.

Page 92

1. trousers
2. customer
3. perfect
4. leather
5. evening
6. elves

1. expensive
2. the amount remaining
3. a place where things are sold

Page 93

sale   crayon   came
they   make   weight
sleigh prey   break
player paint   wait
steak   eighty   day

eighty   hay   skates

1. quickly   5. kindly
2. beautiful   6. helpful
3. happily   7. weightless
4. homeless   8. penniless

Page 94

Stop bugging me! — Leave me alone.

It's raining cats and dogs. — The rain is very heavy.

She has a green thumb. — She's good at making plants grow.

Lend a hand. — Help someone.

That's the way the cookie crumbles. — That's just the way something happens.

You put your foot in your mouth. — You said something embarrassing or stupid.

Stop pulling my leg. — Stop teasing me.

I did it in two shakes of a lamb's tail. — I did it very quickly.

1. called   3. exclaimed
2. asked   4. decided

Page 95
Answers will vary.

Page 98
1. The rabbit heard a noise and thought the Earth was breaking apart.
2. The other animals saw her running and heard her say the Earth was breaking apart.
3. The lion ran in front of the animals and roared at them to stop.
4. The lion made the rabbit go back to the palm tree to see what had really made the noise.
5. The animals learned to find out if something was true before they became frightened.
6. Answers will vary.

Answers will vary.

Page 99
1. scold — to speak sharply to; find fault with
2. nervous — easily excited or upset
3. whisper — to speak very softly
4. noise — sounds
5. coconut — a hard brown fruit of a kind of palm tree
6. wise — have knowledge; make good choices
7. obey — to do as you are told

Page 100
her   world   earth   curse   bird

1. heard   world
2. other   color   purse
3. nervous   turkey   under
4. nurse   work   early
5. smaller   first

Answers will vary.
There are many one- and two-syllable words to choose from.

These are the three-syllable words in the story:
coconut   another
animals   whispering

Page 101
The rabbit thought the Earth was breaking apart. OR The rabbit ran away.

The large animals ran after the hundreds of rabbits.

The rabbit saw that a coconut had fallen to the ground and it had made the noise.

Page 104
1. The little boy was looking for water birds to shoot.
2. The boy saw two tiny men coming down the river in a canoe.

3. The little people wanted to trade one of their bows and arrows for the boy's bow and arrows.
4. The boy didn't think it was a good trade. OR The boy didn't want to trade his bow and arrows for a little bow and arrows.
5. His grandfather said the boy had made a mistake because the little people's bow and arrows would have made him a mighty hunter.
6. The boy learned not to judge people by their size. OR The boy learned that bigger is not always better.

Answers will vary.

Page 105
1. trade — to make an exchange
2. powerful — strong; mighty
3. mistake — a misunderstanding; an error
4. paddle — a short oar used to row a boat or canoe
5. judge — to decide; form an opinion
6. canoe — a light boat pointed at both ends
7. row — to move a boat or canoe using paddles or oars
8. tiny — very small

canoe   bow and arrow   little people

little, small, tiny

Page 106
1. meat   e   6. player   a   11. kind   i
2. smile   i   7. light   i   12. scream   e
3. coach   o   8. paint   a   13. use   u
4. greed   e   9. try   i   14. movie   e
5. follow o   10. though o   15. sleigh   a

Answers will vary.

Page 107
know   bow   heard   bird
tall   small   bean   seen
could   would   why   sky
eleven seven   comb   home
strong along   bough   how

smaller   smallest
faster   fastest
bigger   biggest
tinier   tiniest

1. happiest   3. taller
2. heavier   4. smartest

Page 110
1. Crow and Peacock had been invited to Tiger's wedding.
2. They needed to be more colorful because it was an important wedding. OR The crow was only white and the peacock was only yellow.
3. Crow's idea was to paint their feathers all the colors of the rainbow.
4. Crow painted colorful designs and beautiful pictures all over Peacock's feathers.
5. Peacock didn't want anyone else to be as beautiful as he was.
6. Peacock pretended they were in danger so he could spill the cans of paint.
7. Peacock painted Crow black all over.
8. Answers will vary, but could include: Crow was angry. Crow was upset. Crow didn't want to be friends with Peacock anymore.

Writing will vary.

Page 111
1. artist   4. designs   7. precious
2. pool   5. proud   8. gems
3. harsh   6. moment

Page 112
1. g   5. j   9. g
2. j   6. g   10. j
3. silent 7. g   11. g
4. j   8. silent 12. j

1. hopeless
2. hopeful
3. wonderful
4. harmless

Page 113
1. as yellow as — butter
2. as cold as — ice
3. as hard as a — rock
4. as busy as a — bee
5. as quick as a — wink
6. as quiet as a — mouse

1–6. Answers will vary.

1. but-ter   4. wor-ry   7. let-ter
2. ten-der   5. of-ten   8. in-vite
3. on-ly   6. fun-ny

Page 115
1. The shepherd boy took care of a flock of sheep. OR The shepherd boy watched to make sure the sheep were not harmed or didn't wander off.
2. The shepherd boy was bored because nothing ever happened. OR The shepherd boy was bored because all the sheep did was eat grass.
3. He pretended a wolf was after the sheep.
4. When the wolf really came, the villagers thought the boy was trying to trick them again. OR The villagers didn't believe the boy when he cried wolf.
5. The shepherd boy learned that when people believe you are a liar they don't believe you even when you tell the truth.
6. Answers will vary.

Answers will vary.

Page 116
1. village   4. shepherd 7. munch
2. pretend   5. liar   8. flock
3. ignore   6. tend   9. wander off

1. flock
2. school
3. pod

Page 117
1. unhappy   4. pregame
2. underground   5. uncomfortable
3. preview   6. underpass

1–6. Answers will vary.

village	yell	eagle
city	whisper	jet
state	exclaim	kite
town	shout	dog

Page 118
over–under | give–take | wee–small
full–empty | raced–hurried | front–back
large–big | deep–shallow | noisy–quiet
wept–cried | work–rest | leap–jump

1. sew
2. berries   bear
3. new   doe
4. heel   board

Page 120
1. The sun and the wind were arguing about who was stronger.
2. They were going to try to get a traveler to take off his coat.
3. a. The wind blew as hard as it could.
   b. The sun beamed down on the traveler.
4. The traveler got too hot from the sun, so he took off his coat.
5. Answers will vary.
6. b. Force isn't always the best way to win.

Answers will vary.

Page 121
1. argument   5. declared
2. strolling   6. traveler
3. minutes   7. boulder
4. beamed

1. huge — gigantic
2. beam — shine
3. angry — mad
4. powerful — strong
5. design — plan
6. dangerous — unsafe
7. remain — stay
8. near — close

Page 122
1. ow   6. u   11. aw
2. o   7. ōw   12. o
3. ōo   8. u   13. ōw
4. aw   9. ŏo   14. u̯
5. oo   10. ōō

a traveler | a boulder | an inn
an argument | an hour | an uncle
a coat | a road | a shade tree
an old man | an elephant | a contest

Page 123
The wind blew hard at the traveler.
OR
The wind tried to blow the traveler's coat off.